Brazilian Folktales

World Folklore Advisory Board

BRAZILIAN FOLKTALES

Livia de Almeida and Ana Portella

Edited by Margaret Read MacDonald

World Folklore Series DISCARDED

LIBRARIES
U N L I M I T E D
A Member of the Greenwood Publishing Group

Westport, Connecticut • London

Library of Congress Cataloging-in-Publication Data

Almeida, Livia de.
   Brazilian folktales / by Livia de Almeida and Ana Portella ; edited by Margaret Read MacDonald.
      p. cm. -- (World folklore series)
   Includes bibliographical references and index.
   ISBN 1-56308-930-0 (alk. paper)
   1. Tales--Brazil. I. Portella, Ana. II. MacDonald, Margaret Read, 1940- III. Title. IV. Series.
  GR133.B6A435   2006
  398.20981--dc22   2006000382

British Library Cataloguing in Publication Data is available.

Library of Congress Catalog Card Number: 2006000382
ISBN: 1-56308-930-0

First published in 2006

Libraries Unlimited, 88 Post Road West, Westport, CT 06881
A Member of the Greenwood Publishing Group, Inc.
www.lu.com

Printed in the United States of America

The paper used in this book complies with the
Permanent Paper Standard issued by the National
Information Standards Organization (Z39.48–1984).

10 9 8 7 6 5 4 3 2 1

The publisher has done its best to make sure the instructions and/or recipes in this book are correct.
However, users should apply judgment and experience when preparing recipes, especially parents
and teachers working with young people. The publisher accepts no responsibility for the outcome of
any recipe included in this volume.

CONTENTS

Part 4: Tales of Enchantment

Part 5: Pedro Malasartes, the Trickster

Part 6: Scary Tales

Part 7: Death Tales in Brazil

Part 8: Festival Games and Recipes from Brazil

PREFACE

Livia de Almeida and Ana Maria Portella are Brazilian tellers who perform with the Rio storytelling group Mil e Umas. The name is taken from the thousand and one nights.

Some years ago, storytelling instructors in Rio suggested that tellers did not need huge repertoires. If each teller knew one great story, five or six could do a program. Thus "grupos" were formed, and many, like Mil e Umas, exist to this day. The individual tellers now may have large repertoires, but still they like the camaraderie of performing together.

Livia de Almeida has worked for many years to promote storytelling in the Rio de Janeiro area. She has organized festivals, Tellabrations, and storytelling series in museums and cultural centers. The professional storytelling scene in Brazil is a lively one, and this is discussed briefly in the introduction.

I was fortunate to be invited to Rio's Tellabration in 1998. A hoard of wonderful tellers performed for several days at museums and cultural centers throughout the city. Then a group of us flew to São Paulo for more telling. Livia's full-time job is editor and food critic with the weekly magazine *Veja Rio*, so she used her journalistic and public relations skills to get excellent press for the events.

In 2000 Livia, Ana, and their friend Roberto Carlos Ramos, an amazing Afro-Brazilian teller from Belo Horizonte, visited San Diego to offer workshops at the National Storytelling Association's annual conference, and they also came to Seattle to share stories at schools and libraries. In 2002, Livia and Roberto Carlos were invited to Seattle to perform at our King County Library System StoryFest International. You can read more about Roberto Carlos and his own Afro-Brazilian telling in my *Ten Traditional Tellers* (University of Illinois Press, 2006).

Working with the tellers in their group and with storytelling friends around the country, Livia and Ana have brought together here a delightful compilation of Brazilian folktales. They bring us tales from varying folktale genres and include tales of the rain forest peoples as well as tales from the Afro-Brazilian and Portuguese traditions. Often several cultural influences are found in one Brazilian folktale.

Our book includes forty-six folktales. Here are amazing stories from the peoples of the Amazon, whose unusual tales show motifs not usual in the rest of world folklore. The unique imaginations are fascinating. Some of the other Brazilian tales included here show European influence: "The Bald Chick" is a variant of the Spanish tale "Half-Chick"; "The Princess with Seven Pairs of Shoes" is of course the same motif as the Grimm brothers'

"Seven Dancing Princesses"; tales of the trickster/fool Pedro Malasartes are distinctly Brazilian, descended from Portugal; and several of the tales, such as the two Kibungo stories, are clearly of African origin.

A brief background of Brazilian history and culture is provided in the introduction. Storytelling is very much alive in Brazil today, and information about the storytelling revival among educators and professional storytellers is given at the end of the introductory chapter. Fun festival games and recipes are shared in part 8. For notes about the tales, including motif numbers and commentary, see the appendix.

We hope readers of all ages will enjoy these unusual stories and that storytellers will pass on some of these tales. What a wonderful visit to Brazil they provide. Here are forty-six delightful Brazilian tales to whet your story appetite! Enjoy!

Margaret Read MacDonald

Livia de Almeida and Margaret Read MacDonald
tell stories at Museu de Republica.

INTRODUCTION TO BRAZIL AND BRAZILIAN STORYTELLING

The Country

Brazil, with 8,511,965 square kilometers, is the largest country in Latin America, and the fifth largest in the world. While the rest of Latin America speaks Spanish, the official language in Brazil is Portuguese.

Brazil is crossed in the north by the equator and in the south by the Tropic of Capricorn. Most of the country is located in the tropical zone, but there is a variety of landscapes and ecosystems. The most widely known is the rainforest in the large area irrigated by the Amazon River and its tributaries. It is said that 40 percent of the remaining rain forest in the world is located in Brazil. There is a wealth of vegetable and animal species that still haven't been fully studied.

Brazil is also the fifth most populated country in the world, with almost 180 million inhabitants (2000 census) Most of the population lives in urban areas, especially in the southeast of the country. The capital is Brasilia, right in the central area, but São Paulo and Rio de Janeiro are the biggest cities, with nine million and five million inhabitants, respectively.

Brazilian cities are just like other big cities in the world, filled with high rises, traffic jams, and environmental issues. Like most cities in developing countries, Brazilian cities of today show extreme contrasts. Income distribution is highly unequal. In Rio de Janeiro, for instance, it is possible to see in the same district of Ipanema some of the richest residences in town, while up on the hills are the favelas, with their shacks and cobbled-together brick houses. These favelas often lack running water, electricity, garbage pick-up, and other city services. Among the favela dwellers are many immigrants from the poorer, agricultural areas of the country, like the Northeast.

Brazil's Ethnic Groups

Brazil's official history starts in 1500, when the country was "discovered" by stranded Portuguese sailors on their way to India. At first, Portuguese settlers regarded the new land as a source of riches to exploit and not as a new home. The Portuguese government was more concerned about extracting vegetable and mineral goods from the land than with settling new dwellers. They depended mainly on slaves to work the fields and level the woodlands. At first they tried to enslave the native population. Later, they brought black slaves from Africa to do agricultural work. Present day Brazilians originated from these three very different ethnic groups: Europeans, native Brazilians, and Africans. Our culture is a result of the fusion of different traditions. Brazilian folklore owes its richness to this blend. Oral literature in Brazil shows this great variety, passed from one generation to the other by tradition.

Native People in Brazil

Historians believe that around 1500, the year in which the Portuguese first arrived in Brazil, there were one to three million indigenous people living in the country. After five centuries, the indigenous population has been reduced to 270,000, or 2 percent of the Brazilian population. According to the last official population survey, produced in 2000, the largest concentrations of the indigenous population are in the Northern and Midwestern areas of the country. There are 206 different indigenous nations, some with no more than a dozen members. There are only ten nations with populations over 5,000.

Society and Culture

The various indigenous groups in Brazil hold different customs, sets of beliefs, and organization. But there are a few common traits. They are mostly concentrated in small villages with 30 to 100 inhabitants. They have very rigid laws that establish the way goods are exchanged; the division of tasks; and their beliefs about the structure of the universe, in which there are human beings, animals, and supernatural beings.

Presently there are 170 indigenous languages in Brazil. The most important branch is the Tupi-Guarani, which includes nineteen languages spoken by 33,000 native Brazilians, who live mostly in the tropical and subtropical forest.

The Portuguese language was greatly influenced by the native languages. During colonization, the indigenous languages were spoken as often as Portuguese in the daily lives of the settlers. The Portuguese adopted numerous native words, especially those regarding plants, animals, geographical references, and names. Portuguese only became the language most generally spoken in Brazil some 260 years after the arrival of the colonizers.

The native reserves are, presently, the islands of preservation of the cultures and languages of the native Brazilians. The best known are the Yanomami, located in the states of Roraima and Amazon, where 9,300 natives live, and the Parque Indígena do Xingu, in the Northeast of Mato Grosso, inhabited by seventeen different tribes.

Native Contributions to Brazilian Folklore

During the first two centuries of Portuguese colonization, the native tongue, *Tupy*, was widely spoken. In fact, it was more widespread than Portuguese. It was the language of explorers, settlers, and priests from the Company of Jesus that kept missions all around the new country.

A great of number of tales became part of our tradition through daily contact between the white men and the native population on farms and in the woods. They have been kept alive to this day. Native oral tradition kept track of great deeds done by the tribes' ancestors. It also told a lot about the groups' history, the origins of things, and moral tales, sometimes interwoven with dances and chants. These stories were meant to explain the world, criticize, and educate; fables were shared by the campfire. They were told for fun. Listeners were free to draw their own conclusions.

Native fables have an important place in Brazilian oral literature. However, they have often suffered from misinterpretation. At other times, their terms were subverted to fit religious goals. Even the heroes were changed to meet European standards. Europeans transmitted the native tales according to their personal needs, adapting them to their different ways of thinking and molding the tales according to their own values.

Native Brazilians found explanations for almost any natural phenomenon. The stars, the rain season, the animals, the rivers, darkness of the night, all had a different shape a long time ago. Constellations were born after some tragedy, when animals, children, or men climbed all the way to heaven. The Brazilian Black Bird is the Southern Cross, the most recognizable constellation in our sky. The Pleiades are children who starved after a long famine. Manioc, the native staple food, sprang from the tomb of Mani, a girl with a very fair complexion. Gwaranah, the energetic drink, originated from a dead boy's eye, according to the Sateré-Maué.

In these legends the fantastic is always close, and it is transmitted from one generation to the other, explaining a mythical beginning. There is frequently an epic background. Supernatural elements are a must. In fables, supernatural elements may be present, but they are not typical. These elements are the fabric of legends. Fable is like casual talk, the word that brings joy or sadness. Legend and myth have to do with religious beliefs. They were shared with care and did not become as widely known as the fables. Today they are more frequently found in books or in anthropological works than repeated as a part of oral tradition. They also suffered from misinterpretations, depending on who collected them.

Some very interesting native stories remain quite vital in Brazilian folklore, especially animal tales that involve typical fauna such as monkeys, *jabuti* (a kind of turtle), *urubus* (buzzards), and *onça* (the jaguar, the largest predator in the jungle). The most popular of all is the jabuti (or Yauti, as it is pronounced in the Tupy language). It is a large turtle, much appreciated as food. Short-legged, slow, weak, and silent, the jabuti in the Amazon tradition is like the fox in the European tales. The jabuti is shown as a witty fellow, active and good-humored. He is the kind of guy who has a way with words and likes using them.

African Contribution

African literature, mostly oral, shows some influence of Asia and Europe. The Portuguese and Africans got many tales from the same eastern source. Both African and Portuguese tales often show an Arab influence. Over the centuries, the Portuguese and Africans certainly had the opportunity to share their tales. Many traditional tales spread in coastal communities and moved inland.

The African contribution to Brazilian oral literature includes tales, proverbs, jokes, riddles, songs, and games. The tales, particularly, made a deep impression on Brazilian culture because of the power of the storytellers. In Africa, the storyteller, the *griot*, the *akpalô*, and the *ologbo,* were responsible for keeping the oral tradition. They were to remember all that could not be forgotten. They belonged to a special group with rules, rights, obligations, privileges, and prohibitions. This was a hereditary position. The wisdom transmitted through time made them look a bit magical, soothing and cheering up people, and giving advice. The charismatic appeal of the storyteller shows through expression, gestures and supreme attention to the plot. The Brazilian teller concentrates on the action, suppressing many descriptive details that were present in the Arab tale.

The Brazilian narrator follows a kind of homespun no-nonsense. There is no prison or forgiveness in the end. The criminal loses his life through the judgment of men or kills himself. This is not an Arab element, but very African in its hard way. Generosity, in these folktales, would be an insult to the victim of the wrongdoing, a glorification of the criminals. The audience's pleasure resides largely in punishing the culprit.

In Brazil, the black slave would usually take care of the landowners' children. By this means the slaves spread African tales among the European children, sometimes creating a merging of African and Portuguese cultures. It was the storyteller who put white children to sleep with simple African folktales, many with animal characters: animals that could talk, get married and feast like people. Sometimes they changed the tales, introducing new details, sometimes influenced by the fear that they would never go back to their own land.

Like the akpalô in Africa, in Brazil there were also weavers of tales, the old black servant who could spin wonderful tales and went from one farm to the other telling tales to other slaves. Brazilian oral literature absorbed many tales, especially monkey and rabbit stories. Both characters are endowed with wits, speed, and quick reactions. In these stories, they win through the use of intelligence against strength. The turtle, the stubborn hero that survives in its own slow way with persistence, appears as the hero in hundreds of tales. Often the frog substitutes for the turtle in Brazilian tales. "A Party in Heaven," the story of a land animal who flies to heaven with the help of birds, is one of the most popular of all tales in Brazilian folklore. The story is told about both the turtle and the frog.

African stories are teaming with strange creatures and monsters that eat little children for dinner: the well-known *Bicho Papão,* present even in lullabies; the *Kibungo*; the *Cumunjarim;* the *Tutu Marambaia.*

European Contribution

The Europeans arrived in Brazil with their memories as part of their luggage. Portuguese folktales were introduced by settlers all over the country. Fairies, witches, ghosts, giants, princes and princesses, castles, hidden treasures, foreboding dreams, and the fear of darkness were thus introduced in the young country. There they acquired new shapes. Tales of enchantment, comical stories, animal fables, and religious legends were brought to Brazil. Many Christian legends and myths that came from Portugal were changed as they were transmitted. Lost souls, masses ministered and attended by skeletons, cries, the noise of chains, strange winds, and other surprises came with the Europeans and acquired a regional accent. Oriental motifs had been introduced to Spain and Portugal by the Moors. These tales were changed many times to work as a means of indoctrination for the Catholic faith. Most of the time, the stories that resulted from this process were transmitted orally.

Brazilian folklore is an amazing mix of these many cultures. This story collection offers you a glimpse into these many worlds.

Revivalist Storytelling Today in Brazil

Oral tradition remained alive and well in Brazil during the last century. The presence of the storyteller, sharing whoppers, scary tales, and fantastic adventures, is an everyday fact in most of the country, in villages where electricity remains a luxury. It was in the big cities of the country, where millions of inhabitants are concentrated, that the art of telling stories for a while seemed to have gone out of style. During the materialistic 1980s, with the country shaken by inflation and political unrest, some of the first artists to present storytelling to new urban audiences appeared. One of these pioneers is Bia Bedran, a singer and composer, based in the town of Niteroi, ten miles from Rio de Janeiro, who managed to get a television show on the official educational channel. *Bia Canta e Conta* (*Bia Sings and Tells*) captivated a small but fascinated audience, lasted five seasons, and was a favorite among educators. Bia used puppets and songs to show to young audiences ancient native Brazilian wisdom tales and the funny adventures of Pedro Malasartes.

The present storytelling scene was shaped in the early 1990s. Battling against an ancient problem in the country—illiteracy—Proler, a government agency in charge of reading programs around the country, adopted storytelling as its main tool for stimulating new readers. But where were the storytellers? There was a dire need to develop new professionals as fast as possible and send them across the country performing and, after a while, also teaching storytelling techniques. Under the dynamic coordination of Francisco Gregorio and Elaine Yunes, a university professor and member of Morandubetá, one of the first storytelling troupes, Casa da Leitura do Rio de Janeiro (the House of Reading), became a school for storytellers and also a meeting point for anyone who wanted to hear a good tale. One of the strategies of the Casa da Leitura was to stimulate the creation of troupes. While an individual storyteller would take some time to acquire a repertoire and be able to perform, a group of five or six would be ready very quickly with just one story by each member. All kinds of people got their training there: actors, teachers, librarians, housewives, bank clerks, and students. Literary storytelling was preferred, stressing the importance of memorizing texts word by word, even when dealing with folktales. Storytellers were taught to avoid excessive gestures.

From the Casa da Leitura sprang groups like Confabulando, Tagarelas, Mil e Umas, and Conta Comigo, as well as a few artists who decided to lead solo careers, like Augusto Pessoa and José Mauro Brant. The weekly programs for kids and adults, offered for free, always filled the 100-seat theater built at the back of the Casa da Leitura. During the mid-1990s, the appeal of storytelling in Rio was obvious to producers and corporations. In 1998, with the financial support of SESC-Rio, an association that supports commerce workers, it was possible to organize the first Brazilian storytelling festival, a four-day event with performances, workshops, and the participation of more than twenty groups and artists from Rio and other regions of the country, attended by 4,400 spectators. On opening night Professor Regina Machado, a long-time scholar of oral tradition and sensitive performer from São Paulo, performed. But the spotlight was on a storyteller from Belo Horizonte, an educator who had been himself a delinquent. Roberto Carlos Ramos had been working steadily as a storyteller for over ten years but only well known in his own home state. Presenting his own renditions of the werewolf tale, Roberto showed that he was a master of jump tales.

That same year, the Casa da Leitura helped back the trip to Rio and São Paulo of Dr. Margaret Read MacDonald for workshops and performances during our second Tellabration. On November 21 and 22 there were fourteen performances around Rio, culminating in an open air concert at the Museu da Republica. The next year, our special guest was Heather Forest. The event grew beyond the boundaries of Rio, to Niteroi and Petropolis, where it was organized by Joaquim de Paula, a master musician, puppeteer, and storyteller.

Although storytelling is no longer supported by official reading programs, the city council and culture secretaries occasionally organize events, which are attended by eager audiences. Leia Brasil, a reading program supported by the Brazilian oil company, brings storytelling to schools and educators. Joaquim de Paula and José Mauro Brant have both recorded stories and music on CD. Roberto Carlos Ramos appeared on the most widely seen talk show in the country and has published a beautiful picture book with an audio CD and a CD-ROM. Professor Yunes continues to be involved in the development of new storytellers in her work at Catholic University and the Universidade Estadual do Rio de Janeiro.

Since 2002, Benita Prieto, of the group Morandubeta, has been organizing a yearly international symposium in Rio that draws storytellers from around the world. Regina Ress (from the United States), Lillian Cinetto and Ana Padovani (from Argentina), Ernesto Abad (from the Canary Islands), and many others have taken part in this exciting annual event.

PART 1

MAGICAL TALES OF THE RAIN FOREST PEOPLES

*B*ecause the Amazonian peoples have lived in isolated circumstances throughout the ages, their folktales reveal some astounding themes. Though most of the world's folktales are shared through many countries in various variations, most of these Amazonian tales do not appear elsewhere in the body of world folklore.

THE CREATION OF THE AMAZON RIVER

A long, long time ago, *Jaci*, the silver moon, happened to meet the golden Sun, while wandering by the Amazon forest. The sun was a strong, fiery warrior. As he set his eyes on *Jaci*, the Sun realized that he had never beheld anything so beautiful. They fell in love immediately and decided to wed.

Suddenly the Sun realized that their passion could never be consummated. It would mean the end of the world. The Sun's intense love would scorch all plants and burn all life on Earth. The tears of happiness shed by the Moon would flood the universe. Reluctantly they agreed to part and never meet each other again, for the good of all the world's creatures.

Jaci (jah-cee) the Moon, and Sun never did meet again. Whenever one comes by, the other immediately retreats.

But *Jaci* was so unhappy that she couldn't help but cry night and day. Her tears fell on the forest and filled the valleys. They rolled on down to the sea. In this way the Great River came to be.

STAR FATE OF THE BORORO BOYS

*T*here once lived a very curious little boy in a Bororo village, in the heart of the Amazon forest. It was a time of want. The women, who were responsible for finding food, couldn't find much to eat. One day, one of the older and wiser women from the village suggested that this time they take the little boy.

"They say it is lucky to bring a '*curumim*' (cuh-ruh-mim)," she said. The women agreed.

They left very early, as usual, before the sun rose. It did not take long for them to find a field full of corn. They were delighted and filled baskets with the grain. The next day, they did the same and again found another field full of corn. On the third day, they decided to go to a secret place to prepare the dishes that only fully grown men were allowed to eat.

The boy begged to go with them. At first, they did not want to take him. But he insisted so much that they decided to take him.

"He is just a boy. There will be no harm," they thought.

The boy and the women walked for hours and came to an open spot in the forest. There the women made fire and prepared the dishes that only men were allowed to eat. The boy was overwhelmed by the sweet scents.

"Please, let me try. Just a little," he begged. But they would not let him eat anything.

"You are too small. Wait a bit. In a few years, you too will be able to eat the dishes that only men are allowed to eat, little one," they said, and they laughed.

The boy was very angry. The next day, he stayed in the village, brooding. His friends came and asked him to play, but he remained quiet. He ended up telling them that he had seen the women preparing the dishes that only men were allowed to eat. They were curious. They had heard that they were delicious. He nodded at them. Then he had an idea.

"Let's go to the old woman's hut. Maybe we will be able to convince her to prepare those dishes," he said.

The boys went there. They told everything to the old woman. She remained silent, with her parrot sitting on her shoulder. She nodded, then went outside and brought in the corn. She lit the fire and began to cook many different kinds of dishes. When they were ready, she called the boys. They devoured the food, licking their fingers. When they were full, they

---

went to rest under the shade of a tree. They were content. But all of sudden, a disturbing thought occurred to the little boy.

"What if the old woman tells our mothers that we ate the food that only men were meant to eat? They will be mad at us. They will certainly punish us!"

The boys were uneasy. Punishment would be terrible. This could not happen at any cost. They hurried back to the old woman's house, quite desperate. They begged her not to tell anything. She assured them she would not. But this was not enough for them. They decided to cut out her tongue. Even that was not enough to calm the boys. The old woman would still be able to point at them and show that they were responsible for those terrible actions. So they decided to kill her.

Even then, they found that they were still afraid of the punishment their mothers would inflict on them. The boys were alone in the village with the old woman. More desperate than ever, they decided to make a long, long rope with weeds and climb their way to heaven. They asked a hummingbird to fly higher and higher, and started to climb.

When the women arrived in the village they thought it was very strange that the children were nowhere to be seen. They started to look for them inside the huts, and found nothing, till they came to the old woman's hut. There they found her body and the parrot, who exclaimed: "Boys did it! Boys did it!"

In shock and grief, the women went searching for the children. They were really mad at them. Suddenly, one of them looked at the sky and saw the boys climbing the rope toward heaven. At first they shouted at them very angrily, then threatened them. Then they began to ask them to please come back. They begged, in tears. The children ignored them. So the women decided to follow them, climbing up the rope. But the children were already up in heaven and decided to cut the rope. The women fell all the way down, and when they hit the ground, they became wild cats, howling at heaven.

No one knows for sure what became of the children. Many people believe that they are still up in the sky and that the stars are simply the bright eyes of the Bororo children, shining forever in the night.

HOW THE NIGHT
CAME TO BE

———————

A Tupy myth

*I*n the beginning there was no night at all. Only the light of the day all the time. Night was asleep deep under the waters. There were no animals, and all things talked.

The daughter of the Big Snake got married to a young man. This man had three very faithful servants. One day, he called them and said. "You must leave. My wife does not want to sleep with me." The three servants did what they were told, and the man called his wife to sleep with him. The daughter of the Big Snake did not agree. "No, night has not come yet." Her husband reminded her that there was no night, just day.

"My father keeps the night. If you want to sleep with me, send your servants to the big river to find it."

The young man called his servants again. He told them that they should go to the Big Snake's house and bring back a special coconut for his wife. When they arrived there, Big Snake gave them a basket with the coconut inside and said, "Here it is. Do not open this coconut, otherwise, all things may be lost forever."

The servants started the return trip. However, they were constantly haunted by strange noises that seemed to be coming from inside the coconut. It was the noise of crickets and toads that sang in the night.

After much walking, they couldn't resist any more. They made a fire and opened the coconut.

All of a sudden, darkness was all around.

"We are lost," they despaired. "The daughter of the Big Snake must already know that we have opened the coconut."

They went on their way.

———————

How the Night Came to Be

At home, the girl told her husband. "Your servants have let the night go loose. We must wait for the morning to come." And at that moment, every thing that lived in the woods became animals and birds. The things that rested on the rivers and waters became ducks and fishes. The basket where the coconut was stored became a wild cat.

When the three servants came back, the young man was furious: "You were not faithful to me. You opened the coconut and let the night go loose. The things that were free in the forest, now they are lost forever. From now on, you will become monkeys and you will be doomed to live up on the trees, swinging from one branch to the other."

Part 1: Magical Tales of the Rain Forest Peoples

THE WANDERING HEAD: HOW THE MOON CAME TO BE

A Kaxinawa myth

*A*long time ago, a hunter was walking through the woods when he came upon a gruesome sight. There was a head on top of a long, long stick. It was the head of a man with long hair that flowed in the wind. The hunter thought this might be an evil spirit and decided to run from that place as fast as he could. But then, when he thought about the horrible head, his curiosity overcame him, and he decided to go back. There he found the head again. But this time he looked closely and saw that the head was actually alive! The eyes were shining and blinking. Tears ran from the eyes and fell to the ground.

The hunter went back to his village and called his brothers. They all went to search for the head, carrying arrows, bows, and big wicker baskets. As they ran, they screamed and made a lot of noise to scare away the evil spirits. When they found the head, they freed it from the stick and placed it in one of the baskets. Then they started the long trip back to the village. But the head seemed to be so heavy that it soon made a hole in the basket and rolled to the ground. The brothers chose a stronger basket with a lid and placed the head inside it. But soon the head was rolling on the forest floor once more. They tried to put it inside two more baskets, but it was no use.

Then the men decided to carry the head on their backs. All of a sudden, one of the men yelled wildly. The head had just bitten his shoulder, and it bled abundantly. "Brothers, the head does not want to go to the village. It must be under some kind of spell."

The men decided to leave the head on the ground and continue on their way back to the village. But the head started following them, rolling and rolling.

When the men saw that, they ran, scared. They swam across a deep river. On the other side, there was a fruit tree heavy with fruit. Some of the men climbed the tree to eat and to wait for the head to roll by. The hunter told them, "You can eat as much as you please. The head will never be able to cross the river."

The Wandering Head: How the Moon Came to Be

But the head rolled down the river bank, dove into the river, and swam across the water. The men who were up the tree watched it, terrified. Then the head spoke.

"There is no use hiding. I have seen you up the tree. Throw me some fruit!"

The men picked some green fruits and threw them to the head.

"This is no good!" the head complained, "I want the ripe fruit!"

The men obeyed. They gave the head plenty of fruit. The head swallowed the fruit, but it kept falling through the cut-off neck hole. The head kept asking for more and more.

One of the men had an idea. He told the others to throw the fruit as far as they could. When the head rolled away to grab it, the men climbed down the tree and ran away.

As they approached their village, they began to think that they were free from the head. They didn't notice that it was rolling and rolling behind them, screaming. "Wait for me!" But the men got inside the house and closed the door.

"Open the door, I want to come in!"

Nobody moved.

The head cried, wiping its tears with its long hair and begging to get inside the hut.

After a long while, the head started to think about its own fate. Why should it just terrorize people? Perhaps it could have a better fate. If it became a stream, it would quench the men's thirst. If it became the ground, it would be good to tread on. If it became a house, it would be a shelter. If it turned into flour, it would be good to eat. If it became the sun, it would warm the men when they were cold. If it were rain, it would moisten the soil and make it flourish. After much thinking, the head decided to become the moon.

"I will become the moon. My eyes will be like stars, my blood will turn into a rainbow," the head told the men.

One of the men grabbed the head and wiped the blood off it, and then a rainbow appeared. He tore out both of its eyes and threw them to heaven, and they became stars. A heavenly bird came and grabbed the head by its hair, flying away to the sky.

The people from that village came out of their houses to see. They watched the head hanging by its hair, heading toward the clouds. They saw a rainbow. It got very dark when the head found rest in the sky, and it became the new moon. After that every time the new moon rose . . . the people were bewitched.

The Kaxinawa live in the forests of Acre, by the Iboaqu river.

THE STORY OF MANI

A Tupy myth

*A*long, long time ago, the daughter of a Tupy chief became heavy with child. Her father wanted to take revenge on the man responsible for bringing shame to his family. He used every means he could conceive of to try to extract from his daughter the name of the seducer. But no threat or punishment would work. The girl just repeated that she had known no man. Enraged, her father had her held prisoner inside a hut. He decided to have her killed the next day.

That night the chief had strange dreams that disturbed his sleep. In his dreams he saw a man whose skin was white and shiny like the moon, dressed as a warrior. The warrior looked at him gravely. "You must believe your daughter, for she tells the truth. She has known no man. Take good care of her, honor her, for she is going to bear a great gift to all the people," he said.

The father woke up, startled. He became convinced of his daughter's innocence and asked her to forgive him.

After eight full moons, his daughter gave birth to a beautiful girl, whose skin was white as the moon. She was different from the rest of the tribe. Her dark eyes were shiny and thoughtful. So beautiful was she that people from the neighboring tribes ventured through the forest for days just to look at the child. The girl was called Mani (mah-nee). And Mani grew up really quickly. When she was just a few days old, she was able to walk and talk wisely to all of her visitors. She was loved by everyone who came near her.

However, shortly after her first birthday, Mani died a sudden death, without showing any pain or any signs of illness.

Her grandfather, the chief, was so desolate that he buried the girl inside his own hut. Her mother watered her grave every day, as was the custom among her people.

Some time went by, and one day there sprang from Mani's grave a different kind of plant . . . a plant no one had ever seen before. They let the plant grow, for no one dared to touch it. The plant grew and grew. It bloomed and bore fruit. The birds of the forest that ate the fruit behaved weirdly, as if they were drunk. The people had never seen anything like that. They took great care of the plant, and one day the earth opened and they found a root that reminded them of Mani's delicate body.

The men picked the root from the ground, cooked it, and ate it. It tasted delicious, and it renewed their strength. From this day on, they used that root as their staple food. They also used it to make a drink so strong that it can put a person to sleep. They called it manioc, which in the Tupy language means "the house of Mani," the beloved girl who brought a great gift for her tribe.

THE SNAKE EATER

A Kaxinawa tale

*O*nce upon a time there was a Kaxinawa warrior named Dunu-nuwa. He was a handsome young man, strong and brave, who enjoyed hunting and battling. Dunu-nuwa married Pai, the most beautiful girl of the tribe.

They lived happily in the woods, eating fruit and roots that Pai cooked with loving care. The young man spent his time making bows and arrows. He sharpened the tips of the arrows, and he would choose feathers of the most beautiful birds to make the weapons as beautiful.

One day Pai (Pī) came to him.

"Husband, I don't want to eat vegetables and roots anymore. I am hungry for meat. Please go kill some animal for me."

Dunu-nawa picked his arrows, put his bow across his shoulders and a knife on his waist, and said to his wife. "Go and cook manioc and bananas for us to eat with the monkey I am going to kill for you." And he went to the forest.

The woman was happy, and she started to cook. When the water came to a boil, she put the pot on the floor, so the food would cool. And she waited for her husband to come back home.

When Dunu-nawa was in the heart of the forest, he found many snakes, but he didn't want to kill them. He went on his way carefully. Soon he found a jaguar that had just killed a deer and was about to eat it. With one arrow he killed the jaguar. He tied both animals and went home, dragging his burden.

When she saw the man coming home with so much meat, the woman was happy. The young man said:

"The jaguar had caught a deer. I caught the jaguar. Now go and cook, and eat fast."

After the meal, Pai cut up the rest of the meat and left it to dry. Now she would have meat to eat every day.

Dunu-nawa started to think about the snakes he had not killed. He started wondering:

"Why shouldn't I go back and kill the snakes? I am hungry for the meat of snakes!"

One day he told his wife:

"My wife, I feel like eating river eels. I am going there to catch one."

And he left, carrying his arrows and his knife. But instead of going to the river, he went into the heart of the forest, and he found a huge poisonous snake sleeping under a tree. He killed the snake and cut off its head and the tip of its tail. Then he cut up the meat and wrapped it in fresh banana tree leaves.

He gave the parcel to his wife and said, "I just caught this eel in the river. Cook it fast."

Pai obeyed, and Dunu-nawa started to eat, enjoying every bite. The girl looked at her husband and started to think that this meat was really tasty.

"Would you like to eat some of my eel?" he asked.

"Yes, I would like, my husband!"

And the man offered her a piece of meat. Pai ate it.

"This eel tastes like a snake. Its meat has the stench of a snake," said Pai.

"What is that? There is no stench. It is very tasty!"

But Pai didn't want to eat any more of that. She preferred to eat the dried meat from the first hunt. Her husband became very annoyed because of this.

When the dried meat was all gone, Pai asked Dunu-nawa to go hunting again. The man did just that, and he killed a pig and a snake. He took the fat from the pig. He cut the snake into little pieces, and mixed it with the fat.

When he came home, he said, "I killed a pig and brought you its fat. Cook it fast and eat it."

Pai was happy. She cooked the fat and ate it. But when she ate the fat, she also ate pieces of the meat of the snake. She became ill. She slept many nights, she felt terrible pain, she lost weight and became pale. Her husband asked her:

"Pai, what happened to make you so thin and yellowish?"

"I think it was because of the fat of that pig that you brought me," answered the girl.

Dunu-nawa laughed a lot. Pai was intrigued.

"Husband, why do you laugh at me?"

"You got sick because along with the fat of the pig, you also ate snake meat"

When she heard this, Pai called her relatives and begged them to kill her husband. But the snake eater disappeared, and when Pai died, her death had no revenge.

THE STORY OF THE VITÓRIA RÉGIA, THE AMAZON WATER LILY

*B*y the banks of the Jamunda River, whose waters flow into the River-Sea, hidden in the heart of the forest, there used to live a tribe of brave warriors, whose women fought side by side with the men.

Long ago, the bravest and most beautiful of the women was Caititi (which means New Moon in the native tongue). She lived a happy life. She liked to fish by sunset, when the fish gathered in the middle of the river waters and she could slide her canoe slowly and silently among them.

One day, Caititi was floating in the canoe when she heard a strange whistling sound. She looked carefully at the river banks, and she noticed that, half hidden by the leaves, there was a tall man, with skin as white as the moonlight. He looked like a god, and for a few seconds Caititi stood there paralyzed, imprisoned by that sight. The man took a few steps in her direction. Fast as lightning, the girl aimed her bow and shot an arrow. The white man was wounded in the shoulder and started to bleed. He fell on the ground, looking the girl right in the eyes, as if he wanted to show even through his pain that he wouldn't do her any harm.

Caititi rowed back to her village, leaving behind the wounded man. As she went up the river, she felt in her heart a strange pain that she couldn't explain. The sad eyes of the white man followed her. They seemed to be shimmering on the dark waters of the river, calling her, trying to get hold of her soul, trying to grasp her warrior's heart. Caititi only knew freedom and struggle in the wild of the forest. Frightened, she returned to her village in the darkness, and lay down. But the singing of the night birds, the howling of the wind, and faraway lightning didn't let her forget the man she had left behind.

She couldn't bear the pain in her heart. So she went back to her canoe and decided to search for him.

"He cannot die. His eyes are sweet as the Ruda's singing. His skin is white as the moon and his hair is golden as the sun," she thought.

At this moment, she heard the screaming of a hawk.

"Acauã! Acauã!"

She felt her heart beating faster. This was the bird that announced bad tidings. She was scared.

It was then that the canoe reached the place where she had left the young man. Lightning lit the woods, and she saw him. She approached him, touching him lightly, and he trembled. He was burning with fever. She spoke softly to him.

"Stranger, the arrow that pierced your skin also pierced my heart. I am bonded to you as the stars to the sky!"

Even without understanding her words, the white man held her hands. Caititi took him to a cave, made fire to warm him, and treated his wounds. Soon the young man was sleeping deeply. Caititi stayed at his side the whole night long, noticing that his breathing slowly became quieter. When morning came, she left and, rowing up the river, she went back to her village. From this day on, every afternoon the girl went to the woods to meet the white young man. During the day, her mind would be far away, always waiting for the moment when she would meet him again.

Once he was healed, the stranger spent his days walking around the woods, learning everything about Caititi's tribe: their stories, their uses, their history. In the afternoon, he waited for the girl, who always came wearing the feathers of the urutaí, the bird who has the power to keep the love of those who wear his feathers. But that was a forbidden love. A man from another country, from a people who invaded the forest and enslaved its people, would never be accepted. He would be killed.

In the village also lived a strong warrior, the strongest of them all. He was called Torigo, and he was the son of the leader. Torigo was hopelessly in love with Caititi. The girl used to like him, and in the past they would frequently roam the rivers together. She used to accept his gifts. But after she met the stranger, Caititi avoided Torigo, who was jealous. He suspected that something was happening, and he started to follow the girl around the woods. It didn't take him long to find the lovers' meeting place. He hid himself among the trees and waited till they parted. When Caititi returned to the village, Torigo followed the stranger like a shadow and reached the place where he was camping with other white folks. Soon he realized that the white men had been there spying on the tribe and gathering information to attack them later. Caititi was being used. Torigo went back to the village straight away and told everything he had discovered. The leader gathered his warriors, and they prepared to fight against the white men. It would be a terrible fight. All day they prepared arrows with poisoned tips, and the warriors had their bodies painted. The leader asked Caititi to climb the tallest tree.

"You will be our watch. Your hand will lead our betrayer to his death."

Caititi didn't say a word, but her heart was crying.

"I could never betray my tribe. Never! But how can I kill my love?"

When the battle started, the girl was leading the women warriors. She shot many arrows, but her eyes wandered, looking for her loved one. Suddenly, she let out a scream. She saw her beloved mortally wounded by a poisonous arrow. The fighting was still going on, but Caititi ran to him and lay by his side, with her heart bleeding.

"Open your eyes, my beloved. Say you love me and I will die with you."

She hugged him tenderly. Her pain was unbearable. She dragged his body to her canoe, and she let the canoe float on the waters of the Jamunda to the River-Sea, holding him all the time.

Caité (Cah-ee-teh), the moon, appeared, white and round.

"Caité, Caité," she called to the full moon, "You cannot bring longing to the heart of the man I love. My soul will not live without him. I beg you; change the body of my beloved into the most beautiful flower on the waters."

While she said this, she kissed the young man and gave his body to the depths of the River-Sea.

No one ever heard of Caititi again. But some time later, from the waters of that river there appeared a white flower, more beautiful than any other, floating sweetly on the water. It is the Vitória Régia (Vee-toh-ree-ah Reh-jee-a), the Amazon water lily, which is the symbol of the purest love, and graces the waters of the Amazon River.

The Jamunda or Nhamundá River, an affluent of the left bank of the Amazon River, is full of waterfalls and lakes. It is believed that 400 to 600 years ago there was a kingdom of warrior women living by its banks.

Urutaí is a bird from Para, in the North of Brazil. It is believed that the Urutaí doesn't allow maidens to lose their virtue. With the feathers of their tails, they sweep the ground around the bride's hammock to ensure the girl's purity.

Ruda (Rudah) is a warrior who lives in the clouds. He is the indigenous god of love, the one who cares for the reproduction of all living things. His mission is to make love grow in the hearts of men, making them long for their loved ones and come back to their tribes after wars and wanderings.

Caité (Caiteh) is the full moon. It has the power to make lovers long for their loved ones.

THE HAWK HUSBAND

A Myth from the Sateré-Maué

A long, long time ago, when beasts and people lived together peacefully, there lived a beautiful maiden deep in the heart of the forest. One day, she went to talk to her mother. "Mother, I have not been able to gather enough food by myself. I need a husband who is capable of providing the meat. "That is the right thing to do, my daughter" said the mother. "I have heard that Anaje, the hawk, is searching for a wife. He is handsome and has his home on the top of the hills. His nest is warm and cozy and is always overflowing with meat. He would make a good husband. Go and look for Anajé."

And the girl left her home. She walked and walked till she came to a part of the forest where the trail divided and became three paths. The girl did not know which direction to follow. Finally she found some grey feathers of a bird in one of the tracks.

"This should be the right way. Anajé likes to eat birds such as this."

The girl followed the trail, and after a long time, she met an old lady sitting by a fire.

"Are you Anajé's mother?" she asked.

"Yes, I am," said the old lady.

"I came to marry him."

The old lady, in fact, was only the mother of the gambá (gam-bah), or skunk, an ugly and smelly little animal. This was an opportunity to get her son a beautiful young wife. She decided to deceive the young girl.

"Come on, my darling, hide yourself. My son comes back home in such a temper, you wouldn't want to meet him then.

Later, Gambá came home, bringing birds and eggs. The old lady cooked the meal and started talking to her son. "My dear, what would you do if a beautiful girl came to have dinner with us? How would you treat her?"

"She would be very much welcome. I would invite her to sit with us at the table."

The old lady went to the girl's hiding place and invited her to join them at the table. Gambá was entranced by her beauty and asked her to marry him. But the girl refused.

"You are ugly and dirty. You are not as good a hunter as Anajé."

After they were all asleep, the girl escaped and walked down the road. She decided to follow the second trail. The girl followed the trail, and after a long time, she met an old lady sitting by a fire.

"Are you Anajé's mother?" she asked.

"Yes, I am," said the old lady.

"I came to marry him."

The lady was in fact the buzzard's mother. She decided to deceive the girl, for she wanted a beautiful young bride for her son.

"Come on, my darling, hide yourself. My son comes back home in such a temper, you wouldn't want to meet him then," said the old lady.

Early in the evening, Buzzard came back home, bringing vermin.

The old lady cooked the vermin as if they were little fishes and served dinner. As they ate, she asked her son. "My dear, what would you do if a beautiful girl came to have dinner with us? How would you treat her?"

"She would be very much welcome. I would invite her to sit with us at the table."

The old lady went to the girl's hiding place and invited her to join them at the table. Buzzard was entranced with her beauty and asked her to marry him. But the girl refused.

"You are not Anajé. I would never marry a hunter of vermin."

And the girl left while everybody was asleep. She decided to take the third trail. She walked for a long time. Then she met an old lady sitting by a fire.

"Are you Anajé's mother?" she asked.

"Yes, I am," said the old lady.

"Very good. For I am here to marry him."

"Then, come and hide, my child, because my son always comes back home from his hunts in such a bad temper, that you wouldn't want to meet him then," said the old lady.

Early in the evening, Hawk came back with his game: small green birds. His mother cooked dinner, and they sat down to eat.

"That was a good hunt, my son. It is a pity you don't have a pretty bride to share this meal with us," said the old woman.

"It is true, my mother. I would gladly invite her to sit with us," answered Anajé.

The old woman went searching for the girl in her hiding place. The girl liked the food and the hunter. Anajé also fell in love with the girl. They got married days later, and invited all animals to the wedding party. That is, they invited everybody but the skunk and the buzzard. Buzzard was enraged and jealous, and decided to visit Anajé in his nest and challenge him. He invaded the hawk's home and started searching for the girl, but the hunter was there to defend her. There was a terrible fight, but Anajé had a sharper beaker and stronger claws, and the invader ended up with a deep gash on his head.

Buzzard flew back home, shrieking with pain. He begged his mother to take care of his wounds. The old lady heated a pan full of water, but she was so upset that she didn't realize that the water had come to a boil before she spilled all the liquid on her son's head. The boiling water burned Buzzard and took away all the feathers on his head. He flew away, screaming with pain.

And that is why the buzzard till this day sports a bald head and has never married a pretty girl.

This tale was adapted from versions found in José Vieira Couto de Magalhães, O selvagem *(São Paulo: Melhoramentos, 1935); and Hernâni Donato,* Contos dos meninos índios *(São Paulo: Melhoramentos, 1994).*

Couto de Magalhães registered this tale among natives of the Tocantins River valley, where he lived for four months in 1865 after being shipwrecked by the Itaboca falls. Among the natives, abundance of food is the equivalent of riches, and it seems that, as in other civilizations, the ideal husband is a beautiful, rich, and valiant man.

Anajé is a beautiful, indigenous hawk from the Amazon valley.

THE STORY OF GUARANÁ

*I*n the beginning, there were three siblings who lived in the enchanted forest of Noçoquem. Two were men, and there was also a beautiful girl called Oniamussabe. Onia was the joy of the place, for she was a friend to all creatures. She even mastered the art of talking to the stone. Onia knew which were the plants that were good to eat, and which were good for medicine. She knew where to find seeds to make beautiful necklaces and feathers to make herself even more beautiful than she already was. One day she planted a nut in the ground. It grew into a tall tree that seemed to be scratching the sky. Onia was beloved, and the animals in the forest wanted to marry her, but her brothers were jealous. They wanted Onia just for themselves. They just wanted her to take care of them.

A tiny snake was the first to come forward and show his heart to the beautiful girl. Every day, the snake would let out a perfume so sweet that it made Onia's heart fill with joy and tenderness. One day, the snake dared to look straight into the girl's eyes and wished that she might become his wife. In those days, it didn't take more than looking straight into a person's eyes for people, animals, or plants to get married and procreate. Onia became pregnant, but her brothers were not happy at all. They were in a rage.

"Now she will think only of her child, and she will forget all about us," they said.

They didn't want to see her anymore, and Onia was forced to leave the enchanted place. She built herself a house close to the river and had her child by the waters, surrounded by butterflies. Her child, a boy, was strong and beautiful, and as he grew up, Onia told him all the stories she knew. She told him about her brothers, the enchanted garden of Noçoquem, the animals, and the huge nut tree. And the boy heard these stories so often that as soon as he learned how to talk, he begged her to give him these nuts to eat. Onia tried to convince the boy that this was impossible, for his uncles would never allow that. But the boy insisted, and his cravings touched the mother's heart , so one day she took him there.

They came in secret, but the agouti, macaw, and parrouquette saw the dying embers that they left after roasting the nuts and went straight to the two brothers. They didn't like this news and asked monkey to watch the tree. "If you see any boy, get rid of him," they said.

On the next day, the boy woke up craving those nuts again. But now he had learned the way to the enchanted garden, and he went by himself. He climbed the tree, but Monkey, who was hidden up the branches of a nearby tree, shot him with an arrow. The child fell, mortally wounded.

When Onia discovered that the boy was missing, she went running to the nut tree. She ran as fast as she could, but when she finally arrived, the poor boy was already dead. She cried. But all of a sudden she found unknown strength deep in her heart. "I am going to create a plant so strong, that it will have the gift of healing and giving life back."

So she planted her son deep in the ground. And every day she would come and water his resting place. From the boy's right eye, a plant was born, the guaraná (gwa-rah-nah), which is exactly like a person's eye. The plant grew strong and was filled with fruits. And one day when Onia came to the garden she found her son, strong, happy, and beautiful. This boy, who came from inside the earth, was the first Maué, the source of a proud tribe, the children of guaraná.

This is a myth from the Sateré-Maué. Sateré is their most important bloodline, the one that would generate their leaders. This people used to inhabit the central area of the Amazon state, in the North. They were the first to cultivate the guaraná, a native plant from the area, and turn it into a ritual beverage that is believed to renew life forces and heal diseases.

The guaraná plant has berries that look like human eyes. The natives prepared a beverage with the dried fruit. It has lots of caffeine and supposedly helped them in war. Today powdered guaraná is found in health food stores everywhere. It helps students stay awake and is also a favorite among gym enthusiasts. It is also the name of a Brazilian soft drink.

The Noçoquem is the enchanted place where all the plants and animals that were useful for the Maués are. It is the mythological territory where the tribe lived in the past. The girl Oniamussabe, who knew all the plants and their qualities, was expelled from paradise after being seduced by the snake. Her extraordinary powers and her importance were attributed to her maidenhood. She also created the nut tree. The nut tree is one of the tallest in the forest, frequently reaching over 50 meters (more than 150 feet). These nuts, known as Brazil nuts, are very nutritious and rich in protein.

PART 2

ANIMAL TALES FROM THE RAIN FOREST

*F*or the Amazon native tribes, storytelling gives meaning and order to life. A huge tapestry of tales, myths, dances, and chants was woven by different cultural groups in an attempt to explain the world, the phenomena of nature, and the reasons for certain habits and behaviors and to understand the mysteries that abound in the heart of the forest.

Fables and animal tales, usually shared by adults and children, are tales in which teachings and criticisms can be perceived. These stories remind us of an informal chat. They are meant to entertain and leave the listeners free to wonder and find their own interpretation. Animals are endowed with human traits. It is interesting to note that only those animals that are significant for the Amazon natives appear in their tales. Turtle, for instance, embodies patience, quietness, and slowness, but it is also a strong, resistant animal that does not choose violence as a means of getting its way, but rather hides itself inside its shell when threatened. Because of these traits, turtle was admired by the Amazon men. On the other hand, onça, the jaguar, embodies the impulses, the destructive forces. Onça (on-sah) usually ends the tale covered with ridicule. Though Onça is strong, it is always overcome by the small creatures, whose only resources are intelligence and slyness. Deer, monkey, snake, anta (the largest rodent of the Amazon region), and frog are also common characters in the Amazon tales.

TURTLE AND ONÇA, THE JAGUAR

*T*urtle was slowly crawling her way through the forest when she noticed that Monkey was sitting up in a palm tree, eating fruit.

"What are you doing, Monkey?"

"I am eating the fruits of the Inajá (Ee-nah-jah) tree!" answered Monkey.

"Please, Monkey, would you kindly pick and give me some? They look delicious!"

Monkey laughed, "Why, Turtle? Come on, climb the tree and pick them yourself!"

"But I can't climb trees!" whined Turtle.

Monkey came down the tree, picked up Turtle, and took her to the top of the palm tree, very close to a bunch of fruit. Turtle started to eat hungrily.

"I see you are busy, Mistress Turtle. I am going to take a walk in the forest and I will be back in a minute," said Monkey

Turtle ate to her heart's content and then waited for Monkey. And waited, and waited, and waited. But Monkey was nowhere to be seen. Turtle was starting to get anxious. There was no way to climb down from the tree. Turtle just gazed down . . . too afraid to move . . . scared of falling from the tree and hurting herself really badly.

Then Onça, the jaguar, approached the tree and noticed that Turtle was up there.

"What is that?" Onça was really surprised, "What are you doing up a tree, Turtle?"

"I am eating the fruits of Inajá!"

"Throw some fruit for me! They look so sweet!"

Turtle picked one fruit and threw it to Onça, who kept asking for more and more, till there was no more fruit around Turtle.

"Turtle, why don't you come down the tree?"

"I am afraid of dying!" Turtle was really scared.

Onça, who was still very hungry, decided this cute little turtle could make a really nice dessert. Onça called, "Don't be afraid, my little friend! Just jump. I am strong and I will catch you."

But Turtle was no fool and knew that Onça was not to be trusted. Then an idea flashed through her brain. Turtle shrank inside her shell and threw herself from the branch just like a torpedo. She aimed at the big cat's head. And that was exactly where she landed. Onça fell over dead.

Some months went by, and one day Turtle passed by that same palm tree. There were the dry bones of the Onça. One of the long bones looked perfect to carve into a flute. So Turtle carved herself an Onça bone flute and began to play on it. She was so happy that she sang:

"I've got a flute made from Onça's bones! Ola-la!"

But another Onça happened to be passing by and heard Turtle. It didn't like that story about a flute made of Onça's bones. The big animal decided to investigate.

"Turtle! What is this song you are singing? Did you say your flute was made from Onça's bones?"

"No way! I just said that I got a flute made from the bone of Anta ole-le."

And Turtle immediately hid herself inside a tree trunk. But she couldn't resist temptation and started singing: "I've got a flute that is made from Onça's bones!

The second Onça was furious and started roaring and yelling, "I am going to eat you now!"

But Turtle, smart as Turtle can be, slid away through a hole to the opposite side of the trunk and worked her way away from danger.

Onça spent a long, long time roaring and making threats, until Monkey appeared up a tree, laughing. "Onça, you should be prepared to wait for a long time. Turtle is gone now and will only return in the rainy season."

Furious and frustrated, Onça had no choice but to leave. It was going to be a long time before the rainy season would come.

To use a bone from an enemy's leg and make a flute out of it was an honor to any brave warrior, even among the Romans. Among the Amazon natives, archeologists have found many different types of flutes made with bones from both onças and men. This explains the happiness and pride felt by Turtle as it played its flute: this was Turtle's way of celebrating a rightful victory over a much stronger animal.

HOW AGOUTI (COTIA) FOOLED ONÇA

*C*otia was running like crazy in the forest. This intrigued Onça.

"Where do you go in such hurry, Cotia (Coh-tee-a)?" asked Onça.

"Don't you know? There is going to be a mighty storm with such winds that they may blow all the animals from the forest. I am going home, where I can be safe and warm," answered Cotia, barely pausing.

"Cotia, wait!" Onça was quite anxious. "What is going to happen to me? I have nowhere to go and the winds may take me away! Be my friend, Cotia, tie me to this tree so I won't be blown away."

"Of course, Onça. I will do it gladly."

And Cotia tied Onça very tightly to the tree. Cotia could hardly hide the urge to burst into laughter.

Days later, a termite came by and helped to eat away the ropes that still kept Onça tied to the tree. Onça was so happy that she invited the King of the Termites for a banquet. Cotia, who was close by, decided to make more fun of Onça. Cotia covered its body with honey and went to the termite's home. There the honey-coated Cotia was immediately covered with insects. Wearing this strange disguise, Cotia went to visit Onça. Onça's son announced the arrival of the guest of honor.

"Mom, the King of Termites has arrived, all covered with little termites!"

Onça had prepared a delicious meal, with the best of dishes. The Cotia, in disguise, ate as much as it could. When night came, Onça offered the best bed to the guest. Cotia lay down and slept soundly.

Around midnight, it started to rain. Worried about the comfort of her guest, Onça sent her son to check on the King of Termites. The rain had washed away the honey and the termites had gone away.

"Mom, I went to look for the King of termites, but I found Cotia instead!" said the son. Completely furious, Onça found Cotia sleeping and tied it to a tree.

"Now Cotia, you will have to deal with me! I am going to kill you right now. Dear son, throw Cotia to drown in the pond," yelled Onça. Cotia laughed a lot.

"Thank you, Onça. I am really in need of a bath to wash off the rest of the honey. How gentle of you to think about that! I will love a swim in the pond."

Onça threatened again.

"I have changed my mind. Son, throw Cotia in the thorny bushes, to suffer a slow death!" Cotia started to tremble and cry; it even got down on its knees.

"Don't do that. It will be a horrible death. Have mercy!"

Onça loved to hear that. The big animal grabbed Cotia and used all its strength to throw Cotia in the thorny bushes. But that was exactly what Cotia wanted. As it landed on the ground, Cotia started to run. It ran so fast that it disappeared, and Onça never saw it again.

The agouti (cotia) is a small rodent that lives in the Amazon forest. It is as smart as it is small. It is known to bury the green fruits that fall from the trees and keep them till they are ripe and ready to be eaten.

JAGUAR AND GOAT

*O*nce upon a time, there lived in the forest a jaguar and a goat. Jaguar was tired of living in dirty caves among the woods. She decided it was time to build her own place. A house of her own, just like she had always dreamt of, on a nice plot of land. So she started to search for the right spot. It wasn't very easy to find exactly what she had in mind; however, after a long day she found the perfect spot. "This is exactly what I always wanted: sunny, full of trees, with a creek where I can bathe when it is hot. It is just a matter of weeding and leveling the ground. It will be lots of work. But it will be worthwhile!"

And on the next day, Jaguar worked hard on the plot, cleaning the area, leveling the ground. It was already getting dark when she gathered her tools and left, happy with the results of a hard day's work. "Tomorrow I will start building my own house."

Meanwhile, mister Goat, tired of living with the other twenty goats on a farm, decided to build a house for himself. Goat had always dreamt of living by himself, doing whatever he pleased . One day, he left the farm very early to search for the right spot where he could build his own house. After much searching, he found the perfect spot. "This is so nice! It is exactly what I always wanted, sunny, full of trees, with a creek where I can bathe when it is hot. And look at this, the terrain is already clean! I can start to build the house right away," thought Goat.

He started to work, cutting trees and chopping the wood. By midday, he was exhausted, but all the wood he would need for the house was cut and neatly piled. Goat left, as happy as could be, to get some rest.

Just after goat had left, Jaguar came back. For this was exactly the same plot where Jaguar had decided to build her house. She couldn't believe her eyes when she found all the wood she needed cut and piled. "This is a miracle. Fortune is helping me! Now I will have to raise the walls, but with this help from Above, my home will be ready very soon!" Jaguar worked and worked. She raised the walls and the floor of the house. And she sang and whistled as she worked. She only stopped when night fell. She was tired, but it had been worthwhile: the walls were smooth and shiny, and strong. Jaguar was so proud of herself. She picked up her tools and left to take her well-deserved rest.

On the next day, Goat woke up very early, before sunrise, and went back to work. When he got there, he could not believe his eyes: "Miracle, this must be a miracle! Fortune is helping me!" The walls and the floor of his house were ready. He would have only to

---

build the roof. And he worked the whole morning, really excited. By lunchtime, he had finished the roof. He covered the house with leaves from a coconut tree, tied them tightly with a fine rope, and trimmed the edges, so it would look nice. He worked very carefully, for he did not want any leaks in his new house. He stood for a long time admiring his own work. Now he had to build the windows and the front door. He was a bit worried. "Will I be able to do it? I am so weak and little. Will I be able to do it on my own?" But this was something to be dealt with on the next day. He was really exhausted. He picked up all his tools and went back to the farm to get some rest.

Jaguar arrived just after lunch, full of energy. She wanted to finish as soon as possible so she could move into her new house. But when she arrived at the spot, she couldn't believe her eyes. The roof was ready! She fell on her knees. "Fortune is really helping me. This is a true blessing!" she exclaimed. And she worked harder than ever. Strong as she was, she easily put two windows in place and prepared a sturdy front door. "It is ready!" she said proudly. The windows and the door opened and closed smoothly, without a sound. Jaguar even added handles and locks. But now she was tired. "I must get some rest, but tomorrow, I will paint my house. I think I will be able to move sooner than I thought," thought Jaguar. And she left happily.

Goat left the farm to work very early. When he got there, for a moment he thought he had gone to the wrong place. He could not believe his eyes. "Is this really my house? Two windows, a door, handles and locks! I can only thank fortune. This surely is an amazing miracle!" Now he had to paint the house. He decided to paint the house white, with blue windows and door. And he worked and he worked. But it was worthwhile. The house looked lovely. Goat was happy as could be. "Tomorrow, I can move here. I will only bring my best things. A house like this deserves the best," and he hurried away, ready to prepare his belongings.

Jaguar arrived just after midday and found the house already painted. She couldn't believe her eyes, "What a beauty! And it is painted with blue and white, my favorite colors. Fortune is helping me!" she thought. And she decided to move in the next day.

On the next day, very early, Goat packed all his belongings and left for his new house.

Very early, Jaguar packed her possessions and left the forest.

Goat and Jaguar met in the middle of the road.

"Where are you going carrying all these things, Mister Goat?" asked Jaguar.

"I am moving to my new house, Mistress Jaguar. And where are you going?" asked Goat, very curious.

"I have also built a house and I am moving there right now," answered Jaguar, very proud of herself.

"So I believe we are going to be neighbors. My house is this beauty right here!" said Goat.

"You are wrong, Master Goat, this is MY house. I have weeded, cleaned the plot, raised the walls, and put the windows and door in place," said Jaguar, very angrily.

"But I chopped the wood, did the roof really carefully, and painted the whole house. I kept thinking that Fortune was helping me all the while!" said Goat, enraged.

"I also thought this was a miracle," roared Jaguar.

"And what are we supposed to do now?"

The two animals stood in silence for a while. Jaguar spoke first.

"I believe we must live together, then. But I warn you: I have a terrible temper. If you ever see me frowning, get away from me. That means I am really angry," said Jaguar. She wanted the Goat to feel very frightened and give up the house.

Goat was really scared of sharing the house with Jaguar, but he did not want to give it up. "Ok, Jaguar. I have understood. But take care yourself. If you ever see me sneezing and scratching my beard, get away from me. That means I am enraged!" said he.

And time went by. Each animal tried to keep away from the other as much as possible. But after a week, in the middle of the night, Goat woke up and saw Jaguar standing in the living room, frowning. Nervously, he started to sneeze and scratch his beard. The two of them looked at each other, full of fright. They didn't think twice. Goat jumped through one window. Jaguar jumped through the other window. And they hurried away, running as fast as they could. They were so scared that they are still running away from each other to this day.

HOW TURTLE TRICKED ONÇA

*T*urtle and Spider were partners, and they lived together. One day, Turtle managed to kill a rodent and was cutting up the flesh when Onça came by. Onça immediately offered to help. But much to the disgust of Turtle and Spider, Onça was just nibbling on the meat, rather than helping to prepare it.

Turtle said, "We have a problem. We need fire to roast all this meat, otherwise, it will spoil very quickly!" Turtle thought for a moment and continued. "I don't know what to do. I am very slow and fire is distant. When I get back, all will be lost."

Onça was really enjoying eating all this meat for free. Promptly it offered its services to Turtle. "Don't you worry, Turtle. I am quick and strong, and soon I will be back with lots of fire to roast all this delicious meat. Just tell me where I should go to find fire. Meanwhile, you can keep on preparing the meat."

"Just follow this way," said Turtle pointing toward the setting sun with its small paw. "Do you see that huge ball of fire? That is the way to go. Just run, Onça, and bring lots of fire because we have a lot of meat here."

Onça ran as fast as it could toward the dying sun. It ran and ran, but the ball of fire always seemed to be farther away. Hours later, when the forest was already sunken in darkness, Onça returned, exhausted and disappointed, with empty hands. It was famished and craving to eat the rest of the meat.

But Turtle and Spider had already put away the meat inside their little home. Onça only found some bones.

CRAB WITH THE
FLYING EYES

A Tualipang myth

*C*rab was strolling by the banks of Lake Palaná, the great sea lake. Suddenly, he stopped and said, "Go away, my eyes, go across the lake, my eyes!" And then his eyes were gone. Crab stood there for a moment without any eyes. After a while he said:

"Come back my eyes, come back from the other side of the lake, my eyes!"

And the eyes hurried back to Crab.

Onça, the queen of the forest, had been watching everything, protected by the darkness of the woods. She was in awe! Slowly, she worked her way closer and closer to Crab.

"Here come my eyes!" he said. "I think I am going to send them away once more."

Onça watched him, open-mouthed. She wanted to play just like Crab. "Master Crab, this seems to be so much fun! Tell me what to do!"

"Mistress Onça, I send my eyes to the distant banks of Lake Palaná, and then I order them to come back." explained Crab.

"Please, Crab, do it again!" begged Onça.

"All right. I will do it just once more. Deep in the waters live the *traíra* fishes, with their sharp teeth. They have already sensed my eyes, and are coming closer and closer. They want to eat them!"

Crab sent his eyes across the water once more. "Go away, my eyes, go across the lake, my eyes!"

After a while he said. "Come back my eyes, come back from the other side of the lake, my eyes!"

And the eyes hurried back to Crab.

Onça was amazed.

"Please, Crab, teach me how to do the same! Send my eyes across the big water!"

"No! I can't. The *traíra* (trah-ee-rah) fishes are too close. They would swallow your eyes!" explained Crab.

But Onça would not hear it. She insisted, on and on. She whined, and begged, and when arguments would not be heard, she howled and threatened Crab.

Crab gave up.

"All right. Just keep quiet for a moment. Don't make any noise."

The two animals stood silent for a minute. Then Crab said, "Go away, eyes of Mistress Onça. Go across the lake, eyes of mistress Onça!"

And Onça's eyes left her head, diving into the waters of the big lake. Onça stood blinded at the shore. After a while Crab ordered her eyes to come back. "Come back, eyes of mistress Onça, come back to this side of the shore."

But nothing happened.

Onça started to get impatient.

"Come on, master Crab, why is it taking so long for my eyes to come back?"

Crab called her eyes once more, and once again. But Onça's eyes did not come back.

"I told you. Now the *traíra* fish must have eaten your eyes."

Onça was enraged. She turned in the direction of Crab's voice, ready to eat him. Crab dove into the water and hid himself under a leaf. Onça ran blindly, trying to grab him. She ended up lost in the middle of the forest. Exhausted, she sat on a stone, panting.

That was how Buzzard found her.

"What are you doing around here, Mistress Onça? What happened?"

Onça told him the whole story.

"Please, Buzzard, help me recover my eyes!" she begged.

"Stay right here. I will be back in a minute. I will bring the milk from the *jatoba* (jah-tow-ba) tree," said Buzzard. He left. It took a while for him to come back with two bowls full of milk from the *jatoba* tree, a resin so clear that it looks like glass. Buzzard made a fire and heated the liquid.

"Now Mistress Onça, you must be strong. Don't make a movement. Don't cry. Bear the heat," he said. And he spilled the hot milk into the Onça's right orb. She felt an incredible pain, but did not budge. Buzzard did the same with her left orb. Then he washed Onça's eyes with clear water. Now Onça had beautiful clear eyes that shone like crystal in the darkness of the forest.

"Buzzard, what can I do to show you my gratitude?" asked Onça, happy as could be.

"Please kill a tapir, so I can eat some meat."

Right away Onça disappeared in the forest, and hunted and killed a tapir.

"From now on, Mistress Onça, whenever you kill an animal, you should leave a piece for me. This is fair. I gave you back something that was really precious to you," said Buzzard.

And this is the way things are to this day. Onça hunts so Buzzard can have his share.

The traíra is a carnivorous, predatory fish with very sharp teeth, considered the enemy of the other fishes.

Jatoba is a tree that produces a resin used by native ceramicists to give the inside of the ceramics a glow just like glass. "Its sap is as clear as the Onça's eyes," reported a native storyteller (Koch-Grünberg, Von Roraima zum Orinoco *[Stuttgart: Strecker und Schröeder, 1924] 133).*

CURUPIRA AND THE HUNTER

The Curupira (cuh-ruh-pee-rah) is one of the most fantastic and popular creatures produced by Brazilian folklore. Its appearance varies from region to region, but usually Curupira is three feet tall, bald, with a hairy body. Its teeth are blue or green, and it has big pointed ears. But most important, its feet are turned backwards: the heels are in front and the toes are turned to the back. It is also known to be very strong. If you hear thudding sounds in the woods, you can be sure that they are the Curupira knocking the tree trunks to learn if the trees are healthy or sick. The Curupira punishes those who damage the trees or hunt more than they can eat. With whistles, noises, and false tracks, it makes those who destroy nature become lost in the dark woods.

João was hunting deep in the forest. When the night fell, he could not find his way home. He decided to spend the night under a tall tree. Just after midnight, João was awakened by screams and thudding sounds. He realized that the Curupira must be near. And there he was. Curupira approached João and started chatting. He said he knew João was lost and promised to help him find his way out. But there was a problem: the Curupira was very hungry.

"So am I, Curupira, it has been a long time since I had my last meal," said João.

"Help me and I will help you. Give me your hand to eat," ordered Curupira.

João had managed to kill a monkey. So he grabbed his knife and cut off the monkey's hand.

"I hope you will enjoy it," he said.

Curupira ate hungrily.

"This is delicious. Give me your other hand."

And João cut off the monkey's other hand, and then the feet, and finally the heart. Curupira was delighted with the meal.

"I am satisfied. Now, you can ask me anything!"

João thought for a moment.

"Curupira, I feel so hungry. Maybe you should give me *your* heart to eat."

Curupira opened his chest with João's knife, and took his heart from inside. Then he dropped dead.

João was relieved. When day broke, he managed to find his way out of the woods.

Months later, João remembered the green teeth of the Curupira, and decided to go back and collect them to make arrow points and talismans. He found Curupira's body with the knife still sticking out. So he decided to take the knife with him. But just as he pulled the knife from the Curupira's chest, the creature awoke.

"Thank you for coming back. You show that you really care for me, my friend. I must give you a gift. Take this enchanted arrow with you. Whatever you want, this arrow will give you. You just have to show it to the arrow. You don't even have to use it. But pay attention: never ever show the arrow to anyone. Don't keep it at home, and don't you ever talk to your wife about the arrow."

João became the best hunter in the woods. There was always plenty of meat in his house. But his wife kept asking about his strange change of luck. He had never been so lucky before. And she insisted so much that one day João decided to tell her everything.

On the next day, João went to hunt in the forest as usual. After much walking, he found a large *anta* [a tapir]. He aimed his arrow and shot. But the arrow magically turned into a flying serpent that disappeared in the bushes. Curupira had kept his promise, but João didn't know how to keep a secret. Because of that, the arrow returned magically to its original owner.

PART 3

ANIMAL TALES FROM
AFRICA AND EUROPE

*B*razilians have a delightful tradition of folktales brought by the Portuguese settlers, and an equally exciting tradition brought from Africa with enslaved
people. In this chapter, "A Party in Heaven" and "Monkey and the Corn Cake" are likely of
African origin. "The Cockroach's Wedding" is Arabic, transported through Portugal. And
"Bald Chick" is a Spanish/Portuguese tale with versions told throughout Europe.

A PARTY IN HEAVEN

*T*here was going to be a party in heaven. All the winged creatures were rejoicing, but the earth creatures were sad. They would not be able to go there. However, Turtle, the slowest of all creatures, decided to go anyway. When Turtle announced her plans, the other animals roared in laughter. "Will you fly there? You are so slow you'd better start the trip right now," they joked.

What they did not know was that Turtle had already devised a plan. On the day of the party, she put on her best turtle dress and went to the Vulture's house. The Vulture was busy getting ready to go. He wore a bow tie and had his guitar resting over the bed. Turtle jumped through the window and hid herself inside the guitar. Soon, Vulture started his flight. He was so anxious to get to the party that he didn't notice that the guitar was heavier than usual. When he got there, Turtle waited a bit and then left her hiding place, mingling with the other guests. The birds were surprised to see that Turtle had made it there, in Heaven. All night long, Turtle enjoyed herself. She danced and sang till dawn. But she knew she had to leave by riding inside the Vulture´s guitar. So she hid herself again and waited. When the party was over, the birds started on their way back home. But Turtle was so tired that she dropped asleep and bumped her shell on the bottom of the guitar. Vulture heard the thump and looked inside the guitar. Guess who he found there? Turtle, of course.

"I see this is the way you went to the party in heaven! You will see what I shall do!" Vulture was furious. He turned his guitar upside down and shook till Turtle started to fall.

"If I don't fall,

I won't ever go again to a party at all!"

But she kept falling and falling. She screamed:

"Sticks and Stones, get out of my way.

 Otherwise, I will destroy you!"

But the trees and the stones did not move at all. She hit the ground with her shell. I must say she did not die, because her shell was very hard. It was shattered in a thousand pieces. But the animals of the forest pitied Turtle and helped to find all the pieces and patched her shell till it was whole again. That is why the Turtle's shell looks the way it looks.

THE COCKROACH'S WEDDING

*O*nce upon a time there was a pretty little Cockroach, Dona Baratinha, who found a golden coin as she swept her home. She put the coin inside a box, put a ribbon on her hair, dressed up in her Sunday best, and went to stand by the window of her house. She wanted to find a good husband, now that she had money. A gentle husband who would let her sleep till late morning.

"Who would like to marry Dona Baratinha, who has a ribbon on her hair and money in the box?"

A strong Bull appeared down the road. And she asked:

"Bull, would you like to marry me?"

"For sure!" said Bull.

"What kind of noise do you make during the night?"

"MOO, MOO, MOO!!"

It was too loud. Dona Baratinha put her tiny little hands over her ears. "No, no, no! I don't want to marry you. You are too loud," she said.

Bull left, looking quite sad.

"Who would like to marry Dona Baratinha, who has a ribbon on her hair and money in the box?"

A handsome Horse went by. "I would certainly like to marry you, Dona Baratinha."

"Then tell me, what kind of noise do you make in the night?"

"Hin hinhinhin," said Horse.

It was too loud. Dona Baratinha put her tiny little hands over her ears. "No, no, no! I don't want to marry you. You are too loud," she said.

Next came Rooster, with his red crown. Dona Baratinha sighed. "Who would like to marry Dona Baratinha, who has a ribbon on her hair and money in the box?"

"I would!" said Rooster.

"Then tell me, what kind of noise do you make in the night?"

"I make no noise at all," he said.

Dona Baratinha held her breath, but Rooster was quick to add.

"But I always wake up at sunrise and sing 'Cockadoodle'!"

It was too loud. Dona Baratinha put her tiny little hands over her ears. "No, no, no! I don't want to marry you. You are too loud," she said.

Finally a mouse went by her window. Dona Baratinha sighed. "Who would like to marry Dona Baratinha, who has a ribbon on her hair and money in the box?"

"I would!"

"Then tell me, what kind of noise do you make in the night?"

"I make 'ki-ki-ki, ki-ki-ki,ki-ki-ki'."

"Wonderful. I am not afraid of you!"

The mouse was called João Ratão. Soon they made the arrangements for the wedding, which was going to be followed by a feast. On the wedding day, the priest and all the guests were waiting for the ceremony. Meanwhile, in the kitchen, the ants were preparing the meal: black bean stew. It smelled delicious.

João Ratão was all dressed up, but before the ceremony he decided to go to the kitchen and smell the food. He climbed up the oven to get closer to the pot and couldn't resist. He wanted to eat the bacon badly. As he tried to reach the meat, he tripped and fell inside the pot. João Ratão did not know how to swim. He drowned.

At the church, the bride was nervous. She couldn't understand why her darling Ratão did not show up. She waited and waited. But Dom Ratão didn't come. Desolated, she ordered the feast to begin; she couldn't disappoint her guests. As she started to eat, she noticed something strange in the pot: there was the bridegroom floating, dead.

Poor Dona Baratinha was devastated. Her wedding became a funeral.

But life always finds a way to go on. A few days later, Dona Baratinha found the strength to go back to her window, even though she sang through her tears. "Who would like to marry Dona Baratinha, who has a ribbon on her hair and money in her box?"

THE BALD CHICK

*O*nce upon a time there was a large farm with many hens, roosters, turkeys, and ducks. They had plenty to eat, and there was also clear water for them to drink. All the feathered animals lived happily and harmoniously, like one big family. That is, all but the poor Bald Chick. He was one tiny, skinny, ugly looking chick, with no feathers on the top of his head. The other animals thought he looked weird and avoided him. Bald Chick was always alone, walking with his head drooping, eating what was left of the corn from the fat fowls. The other chicks would nip him with their beaks. They would make fun of him when he was around, laughing at him because of his looks.

One day, when he was looking for food in a garbage pile, Bald Chick found a tiny piece of white paper. "This can only be a letter!," he thought. And then he had an idea.

"I am taking this letter to Our Majesty, the King, and I going to ask him for justice! I can't stand anymore the way I am treated here in this hen house. I am sure that the king will understand my plight and will order me to be served with corn for the rest of my life."

Bald Chick found a sack, put it on his back, and left the farm without being noticed. He walked for a long time, till he found a fox.

"Where do you think you are going, Bald Chick," asked the Fox.

"I am going to take this letter to the King, and I am begging him for justice!"

"Take me along, Chick. I have always wanted to see the King. Everybody says that the palace is beautiful."

"Sure, Fox. Get into the bag, and we will go together to see the King."

And the Fox did what she had been told. She found a cozy spot in the sack. And they both went on their way to see the palace. The chick walked for a long time, till he had to cross a wide river. He was disheartened. He sat on the bank and wondered how he was going to get to the other side.

"I am never going to make it. It is deep, and there are lots of undercurrents, and I don't know how to swim."

All of a sudden he heard a deep voice.

"Where do you think you are going, Bald Chick?"

Bald Chick looked around and realized that it was the River himself who was speaking to him.

"I am going to take this letter to the King, and beg him for justice."

"Would you take me along? I have been here for so long, I would like so much to see different places and visit the palace. I have heard that it is a beautiful palace."

"Okay, I will take you along, but you must fold yourself so many times that you become small. Then you can get inside the sack. But be really careful with the Fox. She must be kept dry."

The River did exactly what the Chick had told him. He folded himself so many times that he became small, like a water ball. He found a spot in the sack. And off they went to the palace. The Chick walked for a long time. They were far away from the farm when the road was blocked by a thorn bush. The Chick stopped. He couldn't find a way to cross it.

But then the Thorn Bush spoke to him.

"Where do you think you are going, Bald Chick?"

"I am going to take this letter to the King and beg him for justice!"

"Would you take me along? I have always wanted to visit the palace!"

"I will take you with me. But first, you must fold yourself till you get really little. Then you can get into the sack. But be careful not to prick the Fox and the River, for they are both inside."

The Thorn Bush did exactly what the Chick had told him. He folded himself so many times that he became small like a thorn ball. He found a spot in the sack, by the Fox and the River. And off they went, the four travelers, longing to see the palace of the King. The Chick walked for a long time, and finally they arrived. The entrance was protected by many guards. The Chick put his head up proudly, and yelled at the top of his lungs.

"I have a letter for His Majesty, the King; please let me in!"

Of course, the soldiers didn't let him in. In fact, they showed their weapons, preventing him from going on. The Bald Chick became quite nervous and started to yell and make a true riot. Annoyed by all the noise, the King came to the window to see what was happening.

"Who is the one who dares to make such a racket under the Royal Window? Who is the one who dares to disturb the Royal Sleep?"

"It is that chick, your Majesty. He keeps saying he has a letter for your Royal Highness," answered the soldiers.

"So let him in!"

Bald Chick entered the palace, carrying the sack on his back, as always. He was shown the throne room, where the King was waiting for him. Pleased with himself, he handed the king the tiny piece of paper he had found in the garbage.

"What is that?" exclaimed the king. "This is no letter. This is just a dirty piece of paper. How does this Chick dare to come in and waste my time? Send this bird to the Royal Hen House, immediately!"

When the Bald Chick got in the Royal Hen House, he was surrounded by nervous hens, upset roosters, and mean chicks that tried to bite him. Bald Chick could only try to run away, flapping his wings, not knowing what to do to escape those beasts.

From the sack, there came a familiar voice.

"Chick, let me out now and I will help you."

The Chick opened the sack, and out jumped the Fox. She was particularly hungry after that long journey, and she started to devour all the royal roosters, hens, chicks, and ducks. Soon the hen house looked more like a battlefield, with no survivors but the Chick. When fox was finished, she dug a hole near the fence, and helped the chick escape, carrying his sack, inside of which there were still the River and the Thorn Bush. The Chick ran all night, but his short legs would not take him too far.

On the following morning, the Royal Cook went to the hen house to choose some birds for lunch. He found none of them alive. He ran to the King to give him the dreadful news.

"That Chick is the one to be blamed for this tragedy," said the King, "I want all of my soldiers after this criminal. I want this Chick here, dead or alive."

The Bald Chick was already far away, but the army, on horses, was much faster than he. He ran and ran, but the soldiers were getting closer and closer. He was despairing. He was sure that he would be caught at any minute. Then he heard a deep voice coming from the sack.

"Chick, let me go. Let me go, because I can help you."

The Chick opened the sack, and from the inside jumped out a little water ball, which started unfolding, unfolding, until it became a large river again. The soldiers were in such a hurry that they didn't have time to stop when they saw River. Most of them drowned in those icy waters. Some managed to escape and reach the other bank. The ones who were not caught by the waters took a long time building bridges and boats, and when they finally crossed the River, the Chick was already far away. They started to hunt for the Chick as soon as they had crossed to the other side. Though the Chick ran as fast as he could, the soldiers, with their long legs, were almost upon him again. At this moment, Chick heard a voice coming from the sack.

"Chick, let me go. Let me go, because I can help you."

The Chick opened the sack, and from inside jumped a little thorn ball, which started unfolding, unfolding, until it became a large thorn bush. So large, in fact, that it looked more like a wall covered with thorns. When the soldiers came running after the Chick, they only saw the Thorn Bush when it was already too late. They were caught, and screamed in pain, and could not cross it. The ones who came behind tried to cut the branches with knives and swords, but the Thorn Bush was so thick that they failed.

So the Royal Army had to go back to the palace without the Bald Chick. And the Bald Chick had to go back to his former home without being able to brag about the King's good-will. He was ashamed. He went back to the hen house but had problems getting through the hole he had used to escape.

"This hole must have shrunk," he thought. He looked for the corner where he used to hide, when suddenly he was surrounded by smiling young hens, fighting for his attention. None of them wanted to bite him. None of them seemed to be laughing at him. None of them called him Bald Chick.

"Funny," he thought, "I would say that things seem to be definitely taking a turn for better."

"Where is the Old Rooster? I don't see him anywhere," he asked.

"He became a part of last night's stew," sighed one of the most sensitive young hens. "Now you are the head of this hen house."

"Me? But I am just a B . . . ," he stopped short, as he noticed his reflection in a puddle. He wasn't a chick anymore. He had become a beautiful Rooster, with golden and red feathers, and a proud crown on the top of his head. The trip to the palace had taken almost a year, and he had certainly grown up. The Bald Chick was no more. In his place was Valiant Rooster, who became the head of the hen house for many years, and was loved and respected by all the animals who lived there, especially the young hens, who found particularly attractive that slight lack of feathers at the top of his head.

MONKEY AND THE CORN CAKE

One fine day, Monkey woke up early in the morning craving a bite of corn cake. "How delicious! A slice of sweet smelling corn cake, with lots of butter and sugar, right out of the oven! Yellow and savory!" thought Monkey. He sat on the top branches of the mango tree where he had his home. But Monkey had none of the necessary ingredients to bake a cake. He decided he would borrow what was needed from his friends.

First, he visited Rooster, and asked for some corn meal. "My friend Rooster, I will pay you back tomorrow, without further delay. Come and visit me at 11 A.M., so we can chat and eat corn cake together," he promised.

Then he went to visit Fox, and asked her to lend him a sack of sugar. "My friend Fox, I will pay you back tomorrow, without further delay. Come and visit me at 11:30 A.M., so we can chat and eat corn cake together."

He went straight to Dog's house next. Monkey asked Dog to lend him two dozen eggs, and promised to pay him back the next day, at twelve, exactly half an hour after the time he had set up with Fox. Now, Monkey just needed one more thing: milk. He went knocking at Jaguar's home.

"Don't worry, madam. Tomorrow I will pay back everything I owe you and you will still share with me a delicious slice of corn cake. Come to my house at exactly 12:30 P.M." Smart Monkey kept the visits half an hour apart from each other.

On the next day, very early, Monkey prepared two huge corn cakes. He ate one, still hot from the oven, all by himself. The second one he put on the table, waiting for his guests. Then he climbed to the top branch of the tree. He tied a red handkerchief around his head, as if he had a terrible toothache, and waited for his friends.

At 11 A.M., sharp, someone knocked at the door. It was Rooster. Monkey told him to go in, pretending he was feeling terrible pain. "Please, do go in. I am sorry I can't get down to welcome you. I feel very sick. But please, help yourself to a slice of this delicious cake."

Rooster was still enjoying his big slice when Fox knocked on the door. Rooster was scared, but Monkey quieted him down.

"Don't be afraid, my friend Rooster. Hide yourself under the bed, and Fox will not find you there," he said.

Monkey told Fox to go in, explained that he was terribly sick, and invited her to eat a slice of corn cake.

"What a scrumptious cake, master Monkey! I haven't eaten anything as good in a long time!"

Up on his branch, Monkey thanked her for the praise. "Please enjoy as much as you want, my friend Fox. Rooster also appreciated it very much."

"Rooster? You mean Rooster was here?"

"He was here . . . and he still is," said Monkey, pointing to Rooster's hiding place. Fox jumped up and swallowed Rooster at once.

Fox was still picking her teeth when somebody knocked on the door. Monkey gave the warning. "It is the Dog. Hurry, my friend Fox, don't be afraid. Hide yourself inside that closet, fast."

Monkey sounded cheerful as he welcomed Dog to his home.

"Go on in, my friend! I have a terrible toothache, but I want you to try some of this corn cake. It is delicious!"

Dog helped himself to a huge slice and was still munching when he begged for more. "Please, help yourself. Fox also enjoyed that cake so much that she had TWO slices!"

"What? You mean Fox was here?"

"She was here and . . . she still is," whispered Monkey, pointing to the closet where Fox was hiding.

Dog knocked the closet down and gobbled up Fox. He was still picking his teeth when someone knocked on the door.

"Hurry, my friend Dog!" said Monkey, "It is Jaguar. Hide yourself behind that door, quickly!" Dog barely had time to hide when Jaguar came in. Monkey started moaning, complained about his toothache, and offered some cake to Jaguar.

"Enjoy as much as you want, Madam. It is really delicious. If you had not hurried, Dog would probably have eaten it all by himself."

"What are you saying, Monkey? Dog was here, eating your cake?"

"Sure, madam. Look, he is still there behind the door!" said Monkey, pointing to the dog's hiding place.

Jaguar saw the poor Dog, leaped up, and ate him right there.

Later she had the rest of the cake as dessert. When she had finished her meal, she cleaned her moustache, and said:

"Monkey, it is payback time now. Give me back all you owe me. Please hurry, because I am getting sleepy"

"What, madam? What do you want, madam? You come to my house, eat a delicious dog, who had already eaten a fat fox, who had just devoured a succulent rooster. Then you eat all my corn cake. Not a single crumb was left for me. And you still have the nerve, the courage to ask me for your milk back? Come on, madam! Be reasonable!"

Jaguar was in a rage, and she leaped at Monkey. But Monkey was much faster and smarter. He simply jumped to the highest branch of the tree and disappeared into the forest.

PART 4

TALES OF ENCHANTMENT

*T*his section contains delightful Brazilian versions of tales the reader may already know from European tale collections. There are interesting elements introduced in these tales . . . such as an imp in a chest in the "Princess with Seven Pairs of Shoes" and a fish mother who does the laundry in the Cinderella-like tale "The Fish Mother"

THE LOUSE-SKIN CHAIR

*O*nce upon a time, there was a beautiful princess who lived in a faraway kingdom. She was fair as a summer day, with golden locks that shone like the sun. Every day, her maid combed her long hair with a silver comb, and then brushed it with a brush made of bear hairs.

One day, wonder of wonders, the maid found a louse among the shiny locks. The princess, who had never seen something like that, was amazed. "Isn't that an interesting animal? Let's keep it as a pet!"

The maid put the louse inside a silken box. Every morning, the princess would take the louse out to get the morning sun. After a few days, the insect enlarged itself. Soon it had grown so much that the box had become too small to shelter it. The princess put it in a bigger box. But the louse kept growing and growing, till there was no box big enough to keep it.

One day, the king came to visit the princess. When he came to her bedroom, he could not believe his eyes. "What is that? What kind of monster is in my daughter's room?"

The louse was huge. By then, it was about the size of a baby whale.

"It is a louse, daddy! It is just a pet, not a monster."

The king was amazed. "Dear daughter, lice are not fit to be pets. This can be hazardous to your health!" The king did not pay attention to his daughter's protests. He had something in mind. He sent the louse away and had it killed. Then he used its hide to cover a chair.

Next, he called the queen and the princess. "You must keep this secret. I am going to invite all the single young men in the kingdom to come here and guess what animal lent its leather to cover the royal chair. My daughter will only marry someone who is smart enough to guess correctly!"

As the princess was as rich as she was beautiful, soon the news spread everywhere, and a long line of young men gathered near the palace's entrance. The first to arrive were the richer boys, who had studied in good schools and read encyclopedias.

"This is certainly a tapir's hide!"

"Out, you are wrong!"

"I am sure it is alligator's hide!" risked another young man.

"Out!"

"It is elephant's leather," said a nobleman who had just returned from a safari in Africa.

"Out!"

After a while, the farmer boys started to visit the palace.

"It is lizard leather."

"Out!"

Then there came the poor and the miserable.

"It is rat's hide!"

"Out!"

"It is cockroach's hide!"

"Out! How disgusting!"

Hundreds of young men visited the palace, trying to guess what animal had lent its hide to the royal chair. All of them failed. The princess was impatient: where were the bright young men of her kingdom? No one seemed to be smart enough.

Far away from the palace, a poor young man named Pedro heard about the princess. He decided to try his luck. All his neighbors laughed at him, but Pedro did not pay attention. He knew he was smart. He put some meat, a piece of old bread, and a bottle of water in his backpack. He did not forget to pack a woolen blanket: it would come in handy during the cold evenings. All set, he left. He walked the whole day long, and when the evening came he was already very close to the palace. Anyway, he decided to camp and make an early start on the next day. He built a fire to broil the meat and was about to start eating when an old man came by.

"Good evening, my son. Would you kindly spare me some of your meat? I had my last meal three days ago," begged the old man. "Certainly, my friend. Eat as much as you want. It is not much, but it has just been broiled," answered Pedro.

The old man was so hungry, and the meat was so tender, that he only stopped when he had eaten the whole piece. Pedro did not mind. He ate the stale bread. He drank from his bottle and did not forget to offer some to the old man. When it was time to sleep, he picked up his blanket and wrapped himself up warmly. However, he noticed that the old man was shivering by his side.

"Please, take my blanket. This is going to be a very cold night. I am younger and stronger. I can be comfortable with only my shirt as a cover," said Pedro.

The old man thanked him very much and managed to sleep soundly the whole night. At the break of dawn, he was already awake. He looked much younger and healthier. He called to Pedro:

"My friend, I must leave now. But I want to thank you for your kindness and give you a gift. I am giving you three pieces of thread from my clothes. Whenever you are in trouble, burn one. And help will come to you."

Then he disappeared silently into the woods.

Pedro packed and went to the palace. As he arrived, he watched the crowds walking around, climbing up and down the stairs. He got near a sentry and told him that he had come to guess what kind of leather covered the royal chair. He was directed to a long line of young men. Pedro went along, feeling very nervous. As he approached the throne room, he could see the queen, the king, and the beautiful princess, wearing rich clothes. The royal chair was in the middle of the room. As the boys approached, they were urged to take their guesses.

"It is snake's hide."

"Out!"

"Whale's hide!"

"Out!"

Pedro remembered then the words of the old man. He stood by a window and burned one of the pieces of thread, thinking hard : "I want to know what kind of material covers that chair!"

Immediately, in his mind's eye, he pictured a louse.

"This is so absurd. A louse cannot be this size!" But as he could not think of anything better, he decided to trust the old man and risk his luck.

When his time came, Pedro looked confident when the king questioned him. He said with a loud and clear voice:

"This is a louse's hide!"

The king rejoiced.

"You are right! You win!"

Everybody cheered. But the princess was not having any fun at all. She did not want to marry such a poorly dressed young man. He looked dirty and dumb. She turned to the king and whispered in his ear.

"Father, help me! Do not force me to marry such an idiot. I prefer to die an old maid!."

The king did not know what to do. He had to keep his word, but deep inside, he did not want his dear little daughter to marry such a poor, clumsy candidate against her will. Then he had an idea. He called Pedro.

"My friend, you have shown how wise you are. But to marry the princess, you will have to fulfill another task. Tomorrow morning, you will be in charge of 100 rabbits. You must take them for a stroll in the woods. When you come back, early in the evening, you must present the 100 rabbits. If there is a single one missing, you will lose the princess."

Pedro was in a panic. Only a crazy man would take 100 rabbits for a stroll in the woods. In less than a minute, they would be gone.

"I am not giving up now. I am too close to getting married to the most beautiful girl in the world," he decided.

On the following morning, Pedro was awake at dawn. The king's servant brought him a cup of coffee and 100 rabbits. He had barely passed through the palace's gates when those rabbits were nowhere to be seen. All the rabbits had run away. But the boy was not worried. He went to the woods, found himself a nice shady spot, and lay down. When the day began to get old and evening approached, he burned another thread from the old man's clothes and said: "I want to gather all the rabbits so we can go back to the palace."

When he finished the sentence, he found a silver whistle right in front of him. Pedro blew it . . . and was surrounded by rabbits. The little creatures made a line behind the boy, and they all went marching to the palace. And when the evening finally came, the king found Pedro and 100 rabbits, forming a long line just like soldiers. The king could not believe his eyes. He counted the animals: they were all there. For a minute, he did not quite know what to do. Then he said:

"Pedro, my boy, you are really very smart. But I need a confirmation of your talents. I want you to go back to the woods with the 100 rabbits and bring them back in the evening."

This time, Pedro did not worry a bit. He put the silver whistle in his pocket and left early in the morning. The rabbits disappeared among the trees, and Pedro lay down to rest. At noon, there came one of the princess's maids, a beautiful girl, all dressed up.

"Hello, Pedro," she said, "I think your rabbits are so cute! I always wanted to have a rabbit as a pet. Would you sell one to me? I would do anything to get a rabbit!"

Pedro realized right away that the girl had been sent by the princess herself as a distraction. The princess would do anything to prevent him from fulfilling the task.

"I can sell you a rabbit, my lady," said the boy after a while.

"Yes? Name your price!"

Pedro smiled.

"I would only sell if you gave me a kiss."

The maid blushed and kissed Pedro.

"Go on, pick up a rabbit and give it to your mistress with my compliments," said Pedro mischievously.

The maid ran away, holding the rabbit in her arms. When she was almost at the palace, Pedro blew the silver whistle. All of a sudden, the rabbit hopped out of her arms and went back to the boy, quick as lightning.

Desolate, the maid had to tell the princess what had happened.

"You are an idiot! I must send a smarter maid this time. You don't even know how to hold a rabbit!"

And the princess sent another maid to the forest. The second girl did not have better luck: the boy agreed to sell the rabbit, asking two kisses as payment. The maid ran off with the rabbit in her arms. Again Pedro blew the whistle, and the little creature hopped back to him.

"You are also an idiot! This time, I will go myself!"

The princess went to look for Pedro in the forest. She found the boy lying in the shade and started to chat with him. After much conversation, she asked him to sell her a rabbit.

"I brought a box full of jewelry. I will give you everything just for a small rabbit."

Pedro was no fool: he knew that if just one rabbit were missing he would lose. But he said: "I agree, your highness. But I don't want any jewelry. I want your shirt."

The princess was outraged! How could he dare want her shirt! She hid her anger though, imagining that if she agreed she would avoid a disastrous marriage. She hid herself behind a tree, took off her shirt, and gave it to Pedro. She held the rabbit tight in her arms and ran. She was crossing the gates when the rabbit heard the whistle and hopped away. She was so mad that she didn't even look back.

When evening came, Pedro marched back to the palace with 100 rabbits in a line. The king had to admit that he had fulfilled the task once more. But the princess had not changed her mind. She did not want to marry this Pedro. Therefore, the king had to use all of his imagination again and propose one more task. This time, he was sure Pedro would fail.

"Pedro, my good friend, tomorrow I want to introduce you to the court. And to show your abilities to my guests, I want you to bring a bag filled with lies!"

Pedro did not understand.

"A bag filled with lies. How can that be?"

"You have understood pretty well. This is what I want you to bring to the feast."

Pedro could not find any sleep that night. Suddenly, he remembered to burn the last thread from the old man's clothes. "I want to learn how to fill a bag with lies." At once, he heard voices telling him exactly what to do.

Next evening, all the court was waiting for Pedro in the banquet room. Even the servants were allowed to stay and see Pedro fill a bag with lies. The king ordered the boy to approach the throne and gave him an empty bag.

"Come on, fill this bag with lies in front of all these people."

Pedro held the bag with his left hand. With his right hand he made gestures, as if he was picking fruit from a tree. And he started to speak.

"For a cute little rabbit, the princess's maid kissed me to pay the price. Now, is that a lie?"

"It is a lie!" cried the maid who had kissed him once.

Pedro pretended to put something in the bag while saying: "That's one lie in the bag!"

"For a cute little rabbit, another princess's maid kissed me twice to pay the price. Now is that a lie?"

"It is a lie! It is a lie!" said the maid who had kissed Pedro twice.

"The bag is already half filled!" said Pedro enthusiastically, pretending to put more and more things inside the bag.

"For a cute little rabbit the princess gave me her shirt to pay the price. Now is that a lie?"

"This is the world's biggest lie!" protested the princess.

"My king, this bag is already filled with lies!"

"It is true," said the king, "now, we need to know if the princess will finally agree to the marriage."

Pedro looked at the princess. For the first time, he noticed that she was smiling. Clumsily, he asked her. "Would you marry me, beautiful princess?"

The girl looked at him very seriously. She realized that he was really very smart. And she also realized that Pedro was indeed very good looking. She agreed.

The king was very happy with his daughter's decision. The wedding feast lasted three days and nights, and it is still talked about. And I have heard that Pedro became the right hand of the king, who admired his wits. Pedro was beloved by his princess and had many, many children, all of them as beautiful as the princess and as smart as himself.

THE THREE SISTERS AND THE CHILDREN WITH GOLDEN STARS ON THEIR BROWS

*O*nce upon a time, there lived a very poor man who had three beautiful daughters of age to be married. One evening, the three girls were sitting by their bedroom window after a long day's work. They were talking about marriage, and each was giving her vision of marriage.

The eldest said: "If I married a king, I would make him a shirt that could be folded in such a way that it would fit in my palm. But when he put it on, it would cover all of him."

The second one said: "If I married a king, I would make him a shirt so small that it could fit in a pigeon's egg, but once unfolded, it would be big enough to cover his bed."

And then the third one spoke: "Me, if I married a king, I would give him three children: two boys and a girl. And they would each have a golden star on their brow."

What the girls couldn't imagine is that a young king was outside their window, listening to their conversation with attention. On the next day, he sent for the three girls. He fell in love with the youngest and decided to marry her.

The older sisters were green with envy. Soon they started to look for a way to separate the youngest girl from the king. This seemed to be almost impossible, for the royal couple was happy as happy could be.

Soon after the wedding, the queen became pregnant. The king was filled with joy. But this was a time of war, and he had to leave his beloved wife and go to the battlefield. He did not want to leave the queen all by herself, so he asked her sisters to stay at the castle, taking care of the queen.

The envious sisters agreed. " We will take good care of the queen. You may go and feel at ease. When you come back you will meet your beautiful child."

When the time came, the queen gave birth to a boy, as beautiful as dawn, with a golden star on his brow. However, before the young mother could hold her child, the two sisters replaced the child with a green, slimy toad. They wrote immediately to the King telling him that the queen had given birth to a monster. Then they gave the boy to a maid and ordered her to throw the child in the ocean. The woman, who had never seen such a beautiful boy, felt too sorry for the child to obey.

"I can't kill such a beautiful boy. He is certainly a special child," she thought. Then she had an idea. There was a very gentle woodcutter who lived in the forest.

"I am going to leave the baby close to his house. Maybe he will find the child and will take care of him."

At twilight, the woodcutter was returning to his hut when he was intrigued by something shining in the woods. He found the baby with the golden star on his brow.

"What a beautiful boy! He seems to be the child of a fairy!" The woodcutter had no sons and decided to take the boy home and raise him.

The king was desolated when he received his sisters-in law's letter. Soon he came back to visit his wife. He barely talked to her. But when he left, the queen was pregnant again. Once more, the sisters offered their help. The king went back to battle feeling that his beloved wife was being cared for.

After many months, the queen gave birth to twins: a boy and a girl, beautiful as the morning sun, with a golden star on their brows. The envious sisters could not stand that and decided to act as they had done before. They replaced the babies with two toads, even more slimy than the first one, and gave the babies to the maid, ordering them to be killed. Once more they wrote to the king, telling him that the queen had given birth to two monsters.

The maid could not kill the babies. She left the children at the same spot, hoping that the good woodcutter would take care of them, too. And later that day, the man found the boy and the girl with golden stars on their brow, sleeping quietly in a basket. He couldn't believe his good luck and took the babies to his own home.

When the king learned about the two monsters, he was desperate and decided to go back to the castle right away. His sisters-in-law quickly showed him the toads. Irate, the king ordered his queen to be imprisoned. "You promised to give me children with golden stars on their brows. But so far, I have only seen three horrible monsters."

Nevertheless, he still loved his wife deeply. Each day, he became sadder and sadder. He stopped leaving the castle. He stayed by himself most of the time, barely eating, and dressed himself only with white clothes. His sisters-in-law tried to make him look at them, but he did not pay any attention. He cried day and night, and became blind with sadness.

While the king and the queen lived in sadness, the woodcutter lived in happiness with his three children, deep in the forest. He had no idea that these were the king's children. He made three woolen caps for the children, to disguise the bright golden stars and avoid the curiosity of other people. The children always wore them when they went to town. The boys were strong and handsome. The girl was beautiful, soft-hearted, and tender as a flower.

When the people learned that their king had become blind, many came with miracle medicines. It was useless. Only the water from the fountain of life would heal him. No one dared to go there, though. The fountain was enchanted, and those who went there never came back. A reward was offered: "Whoever brings the king water from the fountain of life may ask him anything."

Back in the woods, the woodcutter's children heard the news about the king and the reward. "I will go fetch the king some water from the fountain of life. I will restore the king's sight," declared the eldest boy. "If I am not back in seven days, you can go searching for me."

He left. He walked and walked, up the mountains and down the valleys, till he found an orchard full of apple trees heavy with beautiful red fruit. There ran a creek with crystal clear waters. The boy felt so exhausted, hungry, and thirsty that he grabbed one of the apples and ate it. And then he drank from the creek. All of a sudden, he was turned into a stone statue.

Seven days later, his brother left the woodcutter's hut to look for him. He walked and walked, up the mountains and down the valleys, till he found the very same orchard. This brother also ate a red apple and drank from the creek. And he was turned into a stone statue just like his brother before him.

Seven days passed, and the girl decided to look for her brothers. Before she left, she grabbed a bag and packed some bread and a bottle of fresh water. On the next day, she left before dawn. She walked and walked, up the mountains, down the valleys, till she found the orchard. It was still early and the sun was not yet very warm. The girl sat on a stone, ate her bread, and drank from her bottle. She wandered around a bit, and there she found the fountain of life with its bubbling water!

The girl filled her bottle with the precious liquid and returned to the orchard. She realized that there were two stone statues there that strangely resembled her brothers. She gasped. "These are my brothers! They have become stone statues! What am I supposed to do now?"

Then she had an idea. She uncorked the bottle full of water from the fountain of life and let some drops fall on the stone. The stone statues became her brothers immediately. They hugged their sister and hurried back home.

They arrived home, much to the woodcutter's relief. By now, he was wondering if he would ever see his children in safety again. All of a sudden, there was a knock on their door. It was a poor old lady, all dressed in rags, begging for some food.

"Please come in, my good lady, and have some food and water," invited the woodcutter. After recovering her energies, the old lady noticed the beauty of the three children.

"You've got beautiful children, my good man. And they seem to be as good as you and to love you very much!" she said.

"You are right. They are really special, but they are not my own children. I found them in the woods a long, long time ago, and I have raised them as if they were my own," the woodcutter told the story.

The old lady burst into tears. "I was the one who left these children in the woods, hoping that someone would find them and take care of them. In fact, they are the king's children!" she said between sobs. And she proceeded to tell them the whole story of the evil sisters of the queen and the sadness of the monarch.

When they heard the story, the woodcutter and the children decided to leave immediately and bring the water from the fountain of life to the king. They were shown the king's room. Then the girl washed the king's eyes with the liquid and he recovered his eyesight at once.

The king was very grateful. "Just tell me whatever you want, and you will surely have it!"

The children removed their woolen caps and the bright golden stars on their brows shone more than ever. The woodcutter told the story to the king, and only then did the monarch realize that he was surrounded by his own three children. While they were still crying with joy, the two envious sisters came by and realized what had happened. Fearing punishment, they threw themselves from a window of the tallest tower and died.

The king took the three children to the dungeons, where the queen had been living all this time. There he knelt and begged for her forgiveness. The queen was brought back to the throne room and honored with a festival. The royal family asked the woodcutter to stay with them at the castle, and they all lived happily ever after.

PRINCESS TOAD

*A*long time ago, there lived an aged couple who had three grown sons. The boys were old enough to work and live their own lives. But as they could enjoy a good life at their parents' home, they did not make any effort to make their own living.

Their old father was worried about their future. He called the three young men and said: "Dear sons, it is time you leave our home to make your own living. I will give a horse and a bag full of golden coins to each of you. This is all we have. Leave now, multiply this amount, and come back after a year, bringing a present to us."

The two older sons, who had received the best horses, soon hurried away and arrived in town a few days later. They found work in a beautiful palace and met two lovely girls who would do anything for their comfort.

João, the youngest boy, got an old and sick horse that could only hobble down the road. By the end of the first day away from home, João had to leave the poor creature and continue on foot. He walked the whole day and slept in the evening among the trees, eating whatever he managed to hunt. After walking for many days without seeing any town or village, João approached a very old castle, almost in ruins, half covered with weeds. At first he thought it was empty, but suddenly he noticed that there were lights. Tired and hungry, João knocked on the door. There was no answer. He was about to leave when he heard a hoarse voice:

"Come in, come in!'

As he stepped into the castle, João noticed that it was as ugly and dirty as it looked from the outside. However, he realized that there was a huge dinner table all set with the finest china, golden cutlery, and crystal cups. He found platters with the most exquisite dishes: meat, pies, vegetables, wines, and wonderful sweets that made his mouth water. He heard the same hoarse voice telling him:

"Eat, eat as much as you want, my friend!"

That was all João wanted to hear. He sat down and ate to his heart's content. He was so hungry that he was not even curious to know who was talking to him. After the meal, the same voice directed him to a bedroom, where he found a soft bed covered with clean, soft sheets and feather pillows.

"Rest! Rest as much as you want, my friend!" said the voice.

João lay down and slept soundly till sunrise. When he finally awoke, he found his bath ready, breakfast, and then lunch when he felt hungry, both wonderful meals. He spent the day around the castle, curious about the dust, the spider's webs. There was no one around, no sound besides the hoarse voice that called him at meal times.

At dinnertime, he was sitting by the table when he heard a thumping sound in the corridor. He looked back and realized that there was a huge toad, disgusting looking, dribbling, with bulging eyes that looked at him. He almost fell from his chair.

"Are you afraid of me, João?"

"No, mistress Toad!"

"Then stay here with me. You will miss nothing and will keep me company."

João stayed for a long time in the palace, living with the Toad. They talked a lot, and João would read her the books he found in the library. Sometimes they strolled in the garden and had their meals together. But Toad disappeared every night just after dinner. Sometimes she looked sad, but she would say nothing to him. After a while, João got used to her ugly looks and really enjoyed the company of his friend.

One day, Toad came to him and said:

"Tomorrow you must go back to you parents' home. Don't worry: you will find a black horse ready for the trip. And this is the gift you shall offer to your parents." Toad handed him a small bag, very dirty looking, tied with a dirtier ribbon. João did not know what to do with such an ugly gift, but thanked his friend and put the bag in his pocket.

On the next day, he found the horse as Toad had told him and started the trip to his parents' home.

In the evening, the three brothers were back home, rejoicing in their reunion. They had much to tell each other. The older brothers brought their gifts: bear coats, silk embroidered with gold and silver, leather shoes, and two bags full of golden coins each.

"Look father, we doubled the gold you gave us and kept some so we can get married," they said.

The father was very happy. Then he asked João:

"And you, what did you bring to us?"

Clumsily, the boy gave his parents the dirty little bag that Toad had given him earlier. They were laughing at him when his mother, full of curiosity, untied the ribbon and threw the contents over the table. Out of the little bag poured piles and piles of golden coins, diamonds, emeralds, and pearls. His parents were so surprised that they danced and jumped with joy.

"We are rich!"

The older brothers did not like that at all. They were full of envy and did not talk to João for the rest of the evening. Then their father called them together and said:

"Dear sons, you shall leave tomorrow morning and come back in a year. When you come back, I want each of you to bring a gift made by the hand of your bride."

Next morning, the older brothers left early and then João rode off on his black horse, which could run faster than the wind, till he arrived at the old palace. As he entered the dusty halls, he found his bath ready, the table set, and a comfortable bed, as usual. On the next day, Toad visited him, gentle but uglier, fatter, and slimier than ever. The young man thanked her for the gift she had sent to his parents.

And life went on as before. They resumed their conversations and their afternoon strolls in the garden, and soon a year had gone by. João enjoyed more and more the company of Toad. Hours seemed to fly away whenever they were together. Sometimes he noticed that Toad looked at him lovingly, but he pretended not to see.

One day Toad told him: "Tomorrow you must go back to your parents' home. The black horse will be ready, waiting for you. I want you to give your parents something I have made with my own hands."

And she handed him a small glass with a dented lid, full of a dark liquid that resembled mud. João could not believe his eyes. His brothers would certainly bring beautiful gifts, made by their brides, and he would only have that old thing to offer. But he did not want to hurt his friend's feelings, and he put the glass in his pocket. On the next day, he left early, fast as the northern wind.

As before, he joined his brothers for dinner and they were all happy. After much talk, the older brothers brought out gifts made by their brides. One had made a beautiful pillow, embroidered delicately with golden threads. The other girl sent a rich silken tapestry, with the colors of the rainbow. The parents were enchanted.

"What about your bride, João?" asked his father.

Clumsily, the boy gave them the glass with the dented lid. Everybody laughed.

"What kind of gift is this? Your bride must be ugly as a toad to give this mud as a gift!"

João was hurt. He was about to say that he had no bride, when his mother spilled the contents on the floor. Right in front of them there was the finest linen in the world: sheets, pillows, table spreads, and other things that you only see at kings' palaces. They were embroidered with silken threads with the soft colors of the rising sun. Such a delicate work could only have been done by fairy hands. João's parents marveled and kept praising his bride.

"She must be as beautiful as her work. Now that the three of you have proven that you are able to make a living and have chosen good brides, we can only bless you. We have enough riches to last for the rest of our lives. We want you to be back here in one month so you can be married in our village. We will have a wonderful feast that no one will ever forget. Leave early, as the sun rises!"

After the older brothers left, João rode off on his black horse and hurried back to the Toad's palace. As he entered the castle, he found all he needed, as always. Toad was waiting for him. João realized that he had missed her a lot. Although ugly and slimy, Toad was gentle and sweet. Time hurried by.

One day Toad told the young man. "Tomorrow you must go back to your parents' home bringing your bride."

"But I have no bride," said João with sadness.

"You certainly have! Come on, bring me to your parents' home and let's get married!" João was desperate. How could he get married to such a disgusting Toad? At the same time, he did not want to hurt someone who was so gentle, to whom he owed so much. He realized that he would never dare to make her sad. He finally agreed.

On the next day, João found Toad up on the horse, waiting for him. Around them, he found all the animals that lived in the palace, dogs, cats, roosters, ducks, birds, and even two aged looking owls. The creatures made such a racket that João felt ashamed. They hurried away, followed by that noisy crowd. Toad had trouble keeping herself on the horse. Once in a while, João had to stop to see if she was all right. They were very late.

When João finally arrived, there was a crowd waiting at his parents' home, gathering for the wedding feast. The older brothers did not know what to think when they saw João and the toad. At first, they thought that this was some kind of joke, and when João introduced Toad as his bride, they could not stop laughing. João kept his head up and went to church with Toad, and stayed beside his brothers and their brides. When they were finally married, the newlyweds kissed. João picked up Toad from the ground and smacked her a kiss.

All of a sudden there was the sound of thunder and Toad changed into the most beautiful of princesses. With a smile on her face, she told João that she had been charmed by a witch, together with all of her court. Instead of the animals that had followed them from the palace, João found noblemen and servants, all of them richly dressed, all of them thankful.

At the feast, everybody admired the princess. "She is beautiful!" "They are in love!" "They make such a wonderful couple!" João was filled with joy. He had made his parents happy. They were proud of his good heart and knew that he would be happy for the rest of his life.

His brothers did not share their enthusiasm. They were so envious that they could not enjoy the feast. They went away and never came back. I have heard that, after some years went by, their wives became fat and ugly as toads. But João's princess kept growing more and more beautiful with each passing day.

THE SINGING GRASSES

*O*nce upon a time there lived a widower who had a beautiful and gentle daughter. Close to their house, there lived a widow alone with her own daughter. She often went to visit her neighbor's daughter, bringing her honey cakes. "I wish your father would marry again. Then you would have a mother to take care of you, my love," she always said. The widow treated her so nicely that the good girl asked her father to marry her. He was a bit surprised. "I don't know if this is such a good idea. Today she gives you honey cakes. Later on she may give you bitter things to eat." Nevertheless, the man became enchanted with his neighbor's gentle ways. He ended up marrying her.

It did not take long for the woman to change her ways completely. Soon, the girl's father had to take a long trip. When he was gone, her stepmother stopped giving her sweets. The girl was treated almost as a slave and had to do all the housework.

When all the daily tasks were done, the stepmother always ordered the girl to watch the fig tree to prevent the birds from eating the fruit. There was nothing that her stepmother loved more than figs. One afternoon, the girl was so exhausted that she fell asleep, and the birds ate all the fruit.

The stepmother was mad with rage. She killed the girl and buried her under the fig tree.

When the father came back, the stepmother told him that the girl had run away. He was devastated by the news. Time went by. On the spot where the girl had been buried, the grass started to grow wildly. The man ordered his gardener to cut the grass. The gardener started to do his job. All of a sudden, he heard a voice singing from under the earth:

"My father's gardener,

please don't cut my hair.

My mother combed me,

my stepmother buried me,

for the figs of the fig tree

that the birds have eaten away.

Birds, please, go away."

When the gardener heard that, he went running to the girl's father. The man ordered him to dig right there, under the fig tree. And there appeared his beautiful child, more beautiful than ever, and still alive. The stepmother ran away and was never seen again.

THE GOLDEN JARS

A long time ago there lived a woman who had been married twice. She had a daughter and a stepdaughter. She was sweet and tender to her daughter, but she was mean to her stepdaughter, who was a pretty and kind girl. The stepdaughter had to do all the household chores by herself.

One day the woman left home with her daughter to take a stroll and left the other girl alone in the house, cooking, cleaning, and washing the clothes. There was a knock on the door, and the girl found a very frail looking old lady, begging for fire for her pipe. The girl went to the kitchen and left her alone for just one moment. But the old lady took a golden jar that was on the table and disappeared.

When the girl returned with the fire for the old woman's pipe, she couldn't find the old woman. She immediately noticed that the golden jar, one of her stepmother's favorite objects, was missing. She was scared. She knew she would be severely punished when her stepmother returned. So she decided to go after the old lady who had stolen the jar.

She walked aimlessly until she found a golden bird sitting on a twig.

"Golden bird, have you seen an old woman go by holding a golden jar?"

"I will only answer you if you tend my broken leg."

The girl ripped some fabric from her skirt and rolled it carefully around the bird's leg.

"Thank you, beautiful girl. You should ask the rabbit, who lives right there. He will certainly be able to give you more information."

The girl walked on till she found a big white bunny, with his white hair stuck in the middle of a thorn bush.

"White rabbit, have you seen an old woman with a golden jar?"

"I will only answer you if you help me out of this bush."

The girl carefully helped him to free himself of the thorns.

"Thank you, beautiful girl. You should ask the cow, over there. She will certainly be able to give you more information"

The girl walked on and found the cow tied to a tree, looking sad and dejected.

"Cow, have you seen an old woman with a golden jar?"

"I will only answer you if you bring me some fresh water, for I am really thirsty."

The girl got hold of a piece of bark from a tree and went to the river. She brought fresh water in the rounded bark for the cow to drink.

"Thank you, beautiful girl. Now you should walk on, and on and when you reach the end of the road you will find a straw hut. The old woman lives there. She is not home right now, so you should go in and wait. And while you wait, you should do what your heart tells you to do."

The girl thanked the cow and walked on happily. Everything happened as the cow had told her. She found the house and she went in, but the old woman was not there. While she waited, she found that the kitchen was a mess, with piles of dirty dishes in the sink and garbage on the floor. The girl washed everything, swept the floor, lit the fire, and prepared a good soup for dinner. Then she sat on a chair, and she was so tired that she fell asleep. When the old woman arrived home, she was really surprised. She went looking for the one who had done everything. She found the girl asleep. She pretended to be angry and shook the chair. After scolding her for a long time, she ordered the girl to peel all the string beans that were inside a basket. The girl was not afraid of hard work. She did joyfully the task that was ordered by the old woman. She finished it fast, as if by magic.

The old woman then said: "Comb my hair with your fairy fingers!"

The girl obeyed. It is true that once in a while she would find worms, toads, and even spiders on the woman's head. But she wasn't disgusted, and she only stopped when she had untangled her hair.

The old woman seemed content, and after giving the girl some bread and soup, she handed her a dried string of beans and said:

"I am giving you those beans to pay for your stepmother's jar. When you need anything, pull off one of the beans and make your wish."

The girl thanked her and took her way back home, knowing that her stepmother would never forgive her. When she was approaching home, she decided to try the power of the beans. She broke one bean from the string and said, "I would like to have a rich palace."

To her surprise, a rich palace appeared right in front of her, beautiful and sumptuous as nothing she had ever seen.

Amazed, the girl broke another bean from the string and begged for a carriage. And there was a beautiful carriage made of crystal and gold, with six white horses arrayed in gold and lackeys dressed in red velvet uniforms.

The girl broke another bean from the string and asked for clothes that were fit to be worn in that palace and in that golden carriage. She was immediately dressed as a rich princess, with a diamond crown, emerald necklace, and earrings, surrounded by ladies-in-waiting and servers. In the palace she found chests full of golden coins and jewelry. In the closets, there were beautiful dresses and everything she needed to live there.

Soon the village was talking about a beautiful princess who lived in the richest palace in the area. People commented about her beauty and kindness, and soon the stepmother heard those stories. She was furious about the disappearance of her golden jar and of her stepdaughter, whom she supposed had stolen it from her.

The widow and her daughter liked to hang around rich people, and they decided to pay a visit to the princess. They were surprised to discover that she was none other than the young girl they used to torture so much. The envious daughter wanted to know what had happened, and the girl told her everything.

On the next day, the old lady came to visit the widow's house, begging for fire for her pipe. She was received by the daughter, who was very impatient and started throwing everything she could find at the woman. But as soon as she turned back to get more things to throw, the old woman grabbed the other golden jar that was on the table and disappeared.

This girl was bad. She went after the old woman, questioning everyone she met, but to every answer she got, she would do evil. She threw stones at the bird, pulled the hair of the bunny, and whipped the cow. When she arrived at the old woman's house, she broke all the dishes, spilled everything that was kept in the pans, and put out the fire. She waited for the old woman, and as soon as she came in, the girl started cursing and demanding that the old woman give back the golden jar immediately. The old woman smiled. She had a twisted sense of humor, for she not only gave the jar back to the girl, but she also gave her a dried string of beans so she could ask for whatever she wished. And she told her how to do it.

The girl went back home, happy with the gifts and the luck she had had. When she was getting near to her home, she thought that she wanted her mother to be envious of her and wished for a palace even more sumptuous than the princess's. So she broke three beans from the string at once. But when she opened her eyes, she discovered she was inside a dark cave, surrounded by toads, snakes, and scorpions and other disgusting creatures that wanted to attack her. The girl screamed at the top of her lungs, but no one knew where she was. As far as I know, she may still be there, in that cave.

The good girl married a prince who was as beautiful and kind as herself, and she sent for her stepmother, who was sick with grief after her daughter disappeared. The girl forgave all her wrongs, and they lived together in the castle for years and years, in complete happiness.

THE OLD LADY
IN THE WOODS

*O*nce upon a time there was a very poor girl who found work in the home of rich people. Her parents had died and she had been forced to find a job so she would not starve to death.

One day, the girl was traveling in the woods along with the rich couple and all their servants. A band of thieves came from behind the bushes and attacked the group, killing every one of them. That is, every one except the girl, for she felt the danger and jumped out of the carriage, hiding herself behind a tree. When the thieves went away, carrying all the chests with jewelry, golden coins, and valuables, the girl left her hiding place and realized all the tragedy that had taken place.

"How miserable I am! I have no idea of the way to follow in these dark woods. I will probably be eaten by some wild beast, if I don't die of starvation first!"

She cried and wandered around for a long time, trying to find a road that led to safety. When night came, she was very hungry and sat down under a tree. She was so tired that she decided she would stay there no matter what happened.

Some time later, a white dove came flying toward her, bringing in its beak a small golden key. The bird gave the girl the key and said:

"Do you see that big tree over there? There you will find a door that will open to this key. Inside the tree you will find food and drink, and you will never be hungry again."

The girl did what the dove told her and found inside the tree a bowl with milk and a delicious piece of white bread. She ate till she felt revived. Then she thought out loud.

"At this time, the chickens are already going to sleep. I am so tired. I wish I could find a good bed where I could rest."

Before she finished saying those words, the white dove appeared again, bringing her another golden key in its beak.

"This key will open a door hidden in that other tree. There you will find a good bed."

The girl looked for the second tree and found a nice bed, with sweet smelling sheets and pillows as light as feathers. She fell asleep at once.

On the next day, the white dove appeared for the third time, bringing another golden key.

"Go to that other tree and you will find clean clothes to dress in."

The girl obeyed and found inside the tree beautifully embroidered dresses, sewn with gold and stones, so splendid that not even the king's daughter had anything like that.

And the girl lived happily and quietly for a while in the forest, having the white dove as a friend who fulfilled all her wishes.

One day, the white dove came and asked:

"Would you do me a favor?"

The girl immediately agreed.

The dove explained what needed to be done.

"Well, I am going to take you to a house, and you should go in. Inside the house, by the fire, you will find an old lady sitting in a rocking chair. She will say 'good morning' to you, but you must not answer her, no matter what she says. You should go on your way till you find a door. Open it and you will be in a bedroom. On the table you will find many different rings. Some are wonderful, full of diamonds. Leave them all right there and find the plainest one of all, a simple golden circle. When you find it, bring it to me as fast as you can."

The girl did exactly what she was told. She got inside the house and saw the old woman sitting by the fireplace. The woman greeted her.

"Good morning, my dear!"

The girl didn't answer and went toward the bedroom. The old woman grasped her skirt and tried to stop her.

"This is my house, and no one gets in without my permission."

The girl didn't say a word, and managed to free herself from the old woman's grasp. She went into the room. She found shiny rings all over the table. She searched for the plainest of them all, a simple golden circle, but she couldn't find it. While she searched, the old woman came silently into the room bearing a cage. The girl saw the cage and realized that there was a bird holding the ring in its beak. It was hard to retrieve the ring from the bird in the cage, but she did it, and she went away, running through the woods.

She waited for the dove to appear, but time went on and the bird was nowhere to be seen. The girl rested against a tree, for she was tired. All of a sudden, she felt that the tree was becoming soft and gentle, and its twigs were bending down. Then the twigs enfolded her and turned into two strong arms. The girl looked behind her and saw that instead of a tree, there was a handsome young man standing there.

"You have freed us from the curse of the old woman, who is a wicked witch. She had turned me into a tree, although I could still become a white dove for a few hours every day. While the old woman kept the ring, I could not recover my human shape. I, my servants, and my horses were all turned into trees by the wicked witch."

Soon they all recovered their original shapes. The young man was a prince, and he took the girl to his father's kingdom, where they were welcomed and there was a party to celebrate their return. The young man had fallen in love with the girl, and he asked her to marry him. They had a beautiful wedding and lived happily ever after.

THE PRINCESS WITH THE
SEVEN PAIRS OF SHOES

*L*ong ago and far away, in a kingdom whose name has been forgotten, there was a princess who wore out seven pairs of shoes every night. No one knew how to explain that mystery. The king decided to marry the princess to the man who discovered the answer to that riddle. But he forewarned that those who tried and failed would lose their heads. The young men in the kingdom were all scared. No one wanted to risk his head, even for such a prize.

But there was a traveler named João who had heard about the mystery. And he decided to try his luck. He presented himself to the king and said that he was ready to solve the riddle. His royal highness informed him about all the intricate tortures reserved for those who failed, all leading to a hideous death by beheading. João was not impressed at all. He just asked to spend the night in a connecting room with the princess. When all was set up, João went to his room, where he planned to spend the night and watch all the princess's movements. But the girl had already guessed what he was planning and ordered her lady in waiting to offer João a cup of a tea, which would make the boy sleep heavily. João was no fool. He mistrusted the gentle lady who so kindly offered him a cup of tea, and as soon as she left, he threw the liquid out the window. Then he lay down and pretended he was fast asleep, snoring loudly so the princess would hear him

As soon as the princess was ready for bed, João doubled his attention. He had already noticed that the princess had an iron chest under her bed, and that sometimes you could hear strange noises coming from inside. Around midnight, he heard the princess's voice:

"Calicote, Calicote!"

From the vault came a little imp that kept repeating.

"It is time, princess, it is time. It is time, princess, it is time!"

The princess got ready in a minute, and put six pairs of shoes inside the chest. Including the ones she was wearing, she had seven beautiful, brand new satin shoes.

The imp got hold of the chest and of the princess, and left through the window. João followed them, taking all precautions not to be seen. Outside, there was a golden carriage with six black horses all arrayed in silver and gold. Calicote and the princess took the front seats. João hung on at the back of the carriage, which soon left at top speed.

Suddenly the road cut through a field covered with copper flowers. João reached out and grabbed one, and after looking at it in awe, he put it away in his backpack.

Soon the carriage crossed a field with silver flowers, then one with golden flowers, another with emerald flowers, and then ruby flowers and diamond flowers. It was wonderful. João manage to get one flower from each field, putting them away in his backpack, more and more amazed at that mystery.

Finally, they arrived in the richest palace João had ever seen. It was all lit up, even the gardens, which were covered with even more exquisite flowers than the ones João had collected during the trip. From the halls, there came beautiful music. João looked through the windows and could see the servers and the guests, all richly dressed in silver and gold.

The princess and Calicote joined the other guests and went to the banquet room. Carefully, João managed to climb through the window and hide himself under the table. Once in a while, some guest would let a chicken bone or a turkey bone fall: they were made of silver and gold! João collected them and put them in his backpack.

Once the ball started, the princess didn't stop dancing. And every time one of her satin shoes was ripped, Calicote would run to her, throw away the worn out pair, and take a new one from the chest. João, who was very smart, managed to get one shoe from each pair and hide them away in the backpack.

It was almost two o'clock, when the princess called:

"Calicote, it is time!"

"Yes, princess, let's go!"

And they both got in the carriage, which was waiting for them. Without losing any time, João went back to his spot on the back of the carriage, this time with his backpack full.

And they traveled so quickly that when the clock struck twice, they were all back in their own rooms, and the carriage was gone. Calicote got inside the chest, which was hidden under the bed.

When morning came, the king was anxious to have a solution for the riddle.

"Your royal highness, I will give you the answer tonight, at dinner time. I beg you to provide a banquet and invite all the noble folks in the kingdom."

And the king agreed. Dinner was progressing as usual, when João got up and made a toast to the princess, saying that he had some rich and mysterious gifts for her.

"In which garden would you find copper flowers?" he said as he took a copper flower from his backpack and put it on the table. The princess became pale.

"In which one would you find silver flowers? Or golden flowers? Or emerald flowers?" he said, laying them on the table. "What about golden turkey feet and silver chicken feet?"

The guests were all amazed at such rich gifts, but the princess became paler and paler. And João kept taking things from his sack.

"What about this shoe, your highness? And this? And this one?"

And João took out seven satin shoes and put them in front of the princess, who could not stand any more and fainted.

João ran to the princess's room and got the iron chest. He put it in front of the king and the princess. There was a blast, and from the inside there came a cloud of sulphurous smoke. The princess opened her eyes and exclaimed joyfully:

"I am finally free from the curse of an envious fairy. Since the age of 12, I have been forced to wear out seven pair of shoes every night!"

Everyone rejoiced. All the court admired the courage and wit of João, but no one admired him more than the princess herself. And the king gladly gave the hand of his daughter to the boy. They got married on the next day, and the wedding was unforgettable. And, of course, they lived happily ever after.

THE FISH MOTHER

A long, long time ago, in a land far away from here, there were two women who were friends. One was very rich, and the other very poor. Both had a daughter about the same age. The poor woman's daughter was called Maria, and she was smart, hard working, and kind. The other girl didn't do a thing the whole day long, because her mother didn't want her to spoil her hands with housework.

Every day the rich woman asked the same thing of her poor friend:

"Let me raise your daughter, my dear. You can hardly feed her. I can give her beautiful dresses and a good education."

The poor woman wouldn't even consider it.

"No, my friend, I can't do this. My little girl is everything I have left. We are poor, but we have all we need."

In truth, the rich woman really wanted the girl to work for her and do all the household chores. For a bit of food and a mattress in the cellar, she would have a servant to do the washing, the cooking, and all the cleaning.

After insisting on this idea for a long time, she realized that the other woman would never change her mind. The only way to have the girl at her house would be by killing the mother. One day, very early in the morning, she called Maria's mother to join her on the way to the river, where they could wash the linen together. They left the two girls playing together innocently. Whey they had practically finished the washing, the evil lady took advantage of her friend being distracted for a moment and threw her in the deepest part of the river. The poor woman sank rapidly and was taken by the currents.

When the rich woman got back home, she told the girl immediately that her mother had drowned in the river and disappeared into the dark waters, and that from that day on, she would live with her and her daughter in their house. Maria became sick with grief. She cried and cried, and could not take any food or drink for days. Mother and daughter took good care of her, hoping that she would improve enough to do the housework for them.

Being a hard worker by nature, as soon as she recovered Maria offered to help with the household chores, as a way to repay their kindness. But as the days went by, she was given more and more tasks. She cooked, cleaned the house, fixed the torn clothing, washed, and ironed. She had almost no time to rest, and only had leftovers to eat.

One day she went to the river carrying a heavy bundle of clothes. She was so tired that she lay down to rest and ended up sleeping for a long while. She woke up in a panic, for it was time to go back home and no piece of clothing was clean. She started to cry by the river bank. The placid waters became agitated and formed a whirlpool. Then a huge silver fish popped its head out of the water and said:

"Dear Maria, my daughter, why do you cry? What is the reason for such sadness? I am your mother, the one who was killed by that evil woman, and I am here to do anything for your happiness."

The girl was startled, but she dried her tears and told everything to the fish.

The fish listened and then said:

"Put all the dirty clothes in my mouth, and I will wash them for you."

And that was exactly what the girl did. The fish swallowed everything and disappeared into the river. It didn't take long, then it was back, opened its mouth, and all the clothes came out very well washed, sweet smelling, and almost dry. Maria was happy and relieved, and she thanked the fish. She folded all the clothes and still returned home earlier than usual. The woman was surprised when she saw the good work Maria had done so fast, and found that rather strange. On the next day, she gave Maria a heavier bundle and stayed home waiting to see what would happen.

Maria went back to the river and the fish appeared, took the clothes to wash, and soon was back with everything clean and sweet smelling.

The woman thought that this was all very strange, and she gave Maria even more clothes to wash the next day. But this time, she told her daughter to follow the girl and keep herself hidden, just watching what was going on.

Everything happened as before. When the fish appeared, Maria gave it all the clothes and waited by the river bank. The evil woman's daughter saw everything: the fish swallowing the dirty clothes, diving into the waters of the river, and giving the clean clothes back. She ran home to her mother and told her everything.

When Maria came back, the woman told her.

"I know everything. I know who washes the clothes for you. But now, it is all over. I am going to get that fish and have it roasted. Your good life is over, Maria!"

The girl was desperate and went running to warn the fish before sunrise. The fish then talked to her.

"Don't worry my daughter. I knew that she would try to prevent me from helping you, if she found out about me. Listen to me: when she gives you the fish to cook, take care not to lose any part of it, not even one scale. You should not eat a single bite of it, not even to see if it is salty. When they finish eating, you gather all the spines and the scales you set aside and put everything into a white handkerchief. Then, without anyone seeing, go and bury it all in the gardens of the king. Everything is going to be fine, my daughter," the fish promised.

On that same day, the woman had many nets spread around the river, and she managed to get the fish. She took it home and told Maria to cook it for dinner. The girl cried, but did exactly what her mother had told her to do. Although the woman insisted that she try some of the fish, she didn't have a single bite.

Late at night, she left home unseen and went to the castle where the king lived. She buried what was left of the fish, wrapped in a white handkerchief, in the garden.

On the next morning, when the king opened the windows of his bedroom, he noticed a delightful smell of roses, sweet and tender like he had never known before. He looked at his garden and saw a beautiful rose bush, covered with perfect red roses. He wanted to pick one from the bush to smell, but he couldn't do it. Every time he tried to get one flower, the branch would grow and grow, and no one seemed to be able to reach it. Everyone in the castle tried to pick one of the roses, with no success. The king was surprised and promised a great amount of gold to anyone who managed to pick one of the flowers. He invited all the men in the kingdom to try their luck. No one was successful. Next, the king promised that he would marry any single girl in the kingdom who would get the flower for him. The kingdom was in uproar. All the single girls went running to the garden of the castle. They all tried, to no avail. The rose remained out of reach. When the last girl failed, the king ordered his messengers to visit every house in the country, to make sure that all the girls had tried. When they knocked at the evil woman's door, she answered:

"There is nobody here. Just a dirty, ragged girl, who could never present herself to the king. My daughter and I have already tried, but this beggar who doesn't even have shoes cannot go. She has too much to do around here!"

But the soldiers insisted on taking Maria. When the girl arrived at the castle and looked at the rose bush in the garden, she felt her heart lighten. She knew her mother was there to protect her. She got close to the bush, and the rose bush bent and gave her one of its roses. The king was full of joy, and became happier still when he looked at the girl and noticed her beauty and genteel manners. He told the ladies in the castle to dress her with beautiful clothes and cover her with jewels, like a true born queen.

So Maria married the king, and she became a beautiful queen, generous and kind to all.

PART 5

PEDRO MALASARTES, THE TRICKSTER

*P*edro Malasartes is a key character in the trickster tales told around Brazil. The character probably originated in Europe centuries ago. In sixteenth-century Spain, Pedro de Urdemalas was famous for his tricks and ideas. From Portugal came the name of the Brazilian hero Pedro de Malas Artes or Pedro Malasartes (Ill-doing Pedro). In Portugal, he is shown as a fool who manages to make the best of any situation, mostly by chance or sheer luck. The foolish Malasartes was close to the classic stereotype of the clumsy person, the stupid character who finds his way into comedies and tales of many countries.

The Brazilian Pedro Malasartes is no fool. He is a trickster who uses his intelligence to overcome the powerful, the rich, and the violent. He has nothing else besides his tricks. He never carries a suitcase or a bag. He makes money, but never works. He makes his money by fooling those who want to dominate him. Punishment or remorse is unknown to him. He doesn't fear anything. In his ideal world, there is no place for punishment. Telling lies, he manages to sell what he has: nothing. Malasartes is from the countryside. He lives in small villages or farms, he treads long dirty roads, he cooks and sleeps outside. He is a kind of rebel who refuses to work, to have a boss, to be oppressed, to obey the law. When something gets out of control, he simply runs away. He manages to get the women's attention sometimes, only to provoke the authorities. If he does evil, he does it as innocently as a child. He has something in him of the German Till Eulenspiegel and the French Jean Mâchepied, due to their relationship to social satire against the bourgeoisie and the aristocrats, in this case adapted to the arid Brazilian landscape of the Northeast, filled with farmers and shopkeepers. These heroes cannot be considered immoral. They are truly devoid of any morality (amoral).

Popular characters like Malasartes usually change from one region to the other. They can adjust to different environments and times. Brought from Portugal, Malasartes incorporated the quick wit of the Brazilian, in stories meant to be laughed at.

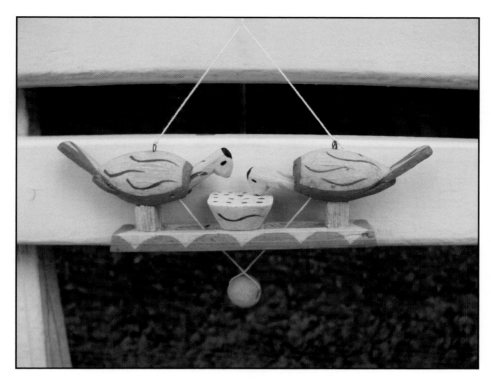

Brinquedos, Brazilian folk toys.

An Amazonian child weaving.

Coconut trees on the coast of Bahia. Coconut trees came from Africa. These became a trademark of Brazil's Northeast. They line the coasts there.

A fishing boat in Boipeba, in Northeast Brazil.

A fisherman in Porto de Galinhas, Pernambuco, in Northeast Brazil.

A carranca (ugly face) carved in wood. The carrancas were used on boats that sailed the São Francisco river to scare away the bad spirits of the waters.

Tapirs lying in the sun in the Rio de Janeiro zoo.

Capybaras eating fruit. This is the largest rodent in the world.

Children snorkeling in Bonito in Mato Grosso, in Central Brazil.

Manioc roots and bananas for sale in open air market.

Reconstruction of a home of the type Brazilian Indians lived in when Europeans first reached Brazil. In the Museu do Indio in Rio de Janeiro.

A view from Olinda, in Northeast Brazil. One of the oldest towns in the country, dating from the sixteenth century.

A folk artist creating a religious image in Minas Gerais, in Southeast Brazil.

A view of Ouro Preto in Minas Gerais, a jewel of seventeenth and eighteenth century, representative of the colonial architecture in Brazil.

Roberto Carlos Ramos telling a "jump" tale.

José Mauro Brandt performing at Museu da Republica.

PEDRO MALASARTES IN THE BAG

*P*edro Malasartes had been playing so many tricks lately, that the villagers were tired of his stories. They decided to make an official complaint to the king.

"Your Royal Majesty, there is a man who says he is not afraid of anyone. He keeps bragging and saying that not even the king would be able to keep him in jail."

The king was furious. He ordered his soldiers to search for the insolent man everywhere. He was to be put in a bag, tied with a knot and then thrown in the ocean.

Six of the king's soldiers soon found Malasartes sleeping under a mango tree, without a care in the world. They grabbed him and put him inside the bag. They tied it with a knot and started climbing to a cliff, so they could throw Malasartes in the ocean.

It was a very warm afternoon, so the soldiers decided to stop at the inn and have a cold drink. They left the bag resting by a tree, near the entrance of the inn. While the soldiers were resting in the inn, a shepherd approached with his flock of sheep and goats.

Inside the bag, Malasartes started to whimper. "How terribly unlucky I am. I don't want it. I don't want it at all!"

The shepherd was surprised. "Who is that inside this bag? Tell me what you don't really want. Perhaps I can help you."

"They want me to marry the king's daughter and I don't want to! I don't want to at all!" cried Malasartes, sounding desperate.

"But I would surely want to marry the king's daughter. I do. I really do!" said the shepherd.

"Then open the bag, so we can change places. You will stay inside the bag and I will leave. When you get to the palace, you will marry the princess."

The shepherd undid the knot and Malasartes got out. The shepherd got in the bag and Malasartes redid the knot carefully, then left as fast as his legs could carry him, taking all the sheep and the goats with him.

The soldiers finished their drinks and came out to hoist the bag onto their backs once more. The man in the bag started to cry. "I have decided, my friends. I am marrying the king's daughter. I will do it!"

The soldiers laughed. This Malasartes man was really hopeless, making jokes even near death. They took the bag up the cliff and threw it into the ocean.

On the next day, Malasartes was seen strolling around the village with his new flock of sheep and goats. The villagers were amazed. They all thought he had been drowned the day before. They didn't understand what was happening.

"Pedro, we saw the soldiers throwing you off the cliff yesterday. How come you are here alive and with so many goats and sheep?"

"You won't believe me, my friends," started Malasartes. "I found these animals in the depths of the ocean. I had never seen so many. The sheep helped me get out of the bag, and they decided to follow me, just like the goats."

The villagers couldn't believe the story at first. But they could see Malasartes, very much alive and with a wonderful flock to prove his tale.

The most ambitious villagers went off running and dove into the ocean. Nobody there knew how to swim. They were all counting on the help of the ocean sheep and goats. But there was no such flock.

PEDRO MALASARTES AND THE DOLL MURDERER

*O*nce upon a time there was an innkeeper who felt he had been cheated by Pedro Malasartes. There was no one so short-tempered or violent in the village as this innkeeper. He wanted to have his revenge. He decided he was going to kill Malasartes with his own hands. He waited till night came, and when the whole village was asleep, he left his home bearing a huge stick. He went straight to Malasartes's home.

The man walked into the house. It was absolutely dark. He opened the bedroom door and could barely distinguish the shape of the person who was lying on the bed. He used his stick mercilessly. He was in such a rage that he didn't realize that there was nothing in the bed but an old ragged doll, just the size of a person. Malasartes was no fool. He knew that the smart thing to do was to stay out of the reach of such a violent man.

When morning came, Malasartes got back home and discovered the beaten up, ragged doll. He stood for a while watching it in silence. All of a sudden, he had an idea. He found his mother's old clothes in the closet. He dressed the doll very carefully. He put a bonnet on the ragged doll, rolled a handkerchief around the neck, and wrapped it with a shawl. He carried the doll, and made it sit upright in front of his carriage and drove slowly to the village inn.

The innkeeper couldn't believe his eyes.

"You!" he exclaimed.

Malasartes pretended not to pay attention to the man's reaction. "How are you, my good man? Isn't this as hot a day as there ever was? My grandmother is napping in my carriage. Would you please bring her some water. I am afraid that she might get sick."

The innkeeper was so confused at the sight of Malasartes that he agreed.

"You must insist," said Malasartes, "the old lady is getting a bit hard of hearing."

The man brought a glass of water outside. At first, he tried to wake up the old woman gently. But she wouldn't say a word. Then he tried to shake her. Finally he lost all patience and started to slap the doll, and hit it harder and harder, till the doll fell limp on the carriage floor.

Malasartes left the inn in time to see what was happening. "What do you think you are doing? Are you crazy? I asked you to bring my grandmother some water, not to spank her!" cried Malasartes.

He examined the doll and started to wail. "What have you done? You have killed my poor grandmother. I am calling the police right now. You will spend the rest of your life in a prison cell, you murderer!" said Malasartes, in tears.

The innkeeper tried to excuse himself. "I didn't mean it, Pedro, but she wouldn't listen to me. I lost my patience. I didn't mean to kill her, Pedro," he whined.

The innkeeper was desperate. He offered Malasartes two bags filled with golden coins to not call the police. After crying a little bit more, Malasartes agreed. He placed the rag doll carefully on the floor in the inn.

"And don't forget to give her a decent burial, too," he said as he jumped back into his carriage and whipped his horses. He was gone as fast as his horses would carry him. And it took a while for the innkeeper to realize that he had been cheated once more by Pedro Malasartes.

PEDRO MALASARTES HERDS PIGS

*O*nce upon a time there lived a man who had two sons, João and Pedro. They were very poor. One day, the man sent João away. "You must find yourself a job; otherwise, we will starve to death." João left and managed to find work at a rich farmer's house. He had to take care of the pigs. After a full month of hard work, the farmer refused to give him any payment. "How dare you ask me for money? My pigs have lost weight. See how the poor creatures look dirty," he complained. João went back home feeling very angry.

"Father, I have been fooled by that farmer. I have worked from morning to dusk, day after day. And I never even got enough food for myself," he said.

Pedro rose from his bed as he heard his brother's grievances.

"Don't you worry, father. Don't you worry brother. I will go back to that farm, and you may rest assured: I will get the money he owes you and much more!"

The old man, who knew Pedro only too well, was concerned.

"I hope you know what you are going to do! Please try not to get in trouble!" he said.

Pedro hated any kind of work. But he hated being cheated even more. He went to the farm and looked for the rich man, begging for a job. The rich man ordered him to take care of seven pigs.

"You must take them to the pastures over the hill. Take good care of them so they don't get lost," said the farmer.

Pedro took the pigs to the pasture. After a while, he met a traveler coming down the road. The man admired his pigs. "These are wonderful pigs. Would you sell me the seven of them?" he asked. Pedro was enthusiastic.

"I am happy you like them. But I can sell you only six pigs. And I must cut off their tails before I sell them to you. But you can take them with you right away."

The traveler agreed. Pedro cut off the tails of six pigs, put away the money, and continued on his way with just one pig.

He walked till he reached a swamp. He stuck the six tails in the mud and half buried the seventh pig. Then he started screaming like crazy.

"You must come and help, master. The pigs have sunk in the swamp. Please help me take them away from the mud. I can't do it by myself!"

The farmer came right away. As soon as he got himself in the mud, he managed to extract from the swamp the pig that was half buried. Then he saw the six tails. He started to pull. And he pulled. And he pulled. And all of a sudden he had one of the tails in his hand.

"Dear master, the pigs are too fat to be pulled by the tail," Pedro looked very seriously at the farmer.

"Go back to the house and ask my wife to give you two shovels so we can unbury the pigs. Hurry, you fool, or the pigs will die!" the farmer ordered.

Pedro flew down the road. He knew that the farmer kept at home two big bags full of golden coins. He never let anyone touch them, not even his wife. Pedro met the farmer's wife in the kitchen.

"Please hurry! Master ordered you to give me the two bags full of golden coins. And he wants them quickly!" said Pedro.

The woman laughed. "Are you crazy? My husband doesn't allow me to touch the bags. He would never give them to you!"

Pedro looked hurt. "Well, if you don't believe me, then ask him yourself," said the boy.

The woman opened the kitchen door. She could glimpse her husband far away in the swamp. "Do you want me to give Pedro both of them?" she shouted.

The farmer was furious with the delay. "Both of them, lazy woman. And hurry!"

The woman did not want to make her husband angrier. Quickly, she picked up the two bags and gave them to Pedro. The smart guy waved good-bye and hurried away from the farm. He had his revenge! And from that day on, nobody at that farm had any idea of what had happened to Pedro, the pigs, and the two bags full of golden coins.

PEDRO MALASARTES SELLS RABBITS

*P*edro Malasartes once bought two rabbits with his few last coins. He stood by the road, wondering what he could do to make some money. After a while, a man walked by. Malasartes had an idea. He showed him the rabbits.

"My good gentleman, you must see these rabbits. I have trained them carefully. They will find any person you order. Would you like to see them in action?" he asked.

The man was really curious. He agreed. Malasartes held the rabbits and uttered: "I want you both to run to Mr. Joaquim's house."

Both rabbits dashed away, running straight to Mr. Joaquim's garden. The man watched everything wide-eyed.

"I need those rabbits right now! Name your price!"

Pedro looked immersed in thought. He pretended that he did not want to sell his dear rabbits. "It is not a matter of money, sir. I have spent so much time and energy training them!"

The man insisted. Finally, Pedro agreed. "I want 20 coins for each one." Now that was a huge amount of money. But the man really wanted the well-trained rabbits, and he agreed to pay the price. He thought he was making a smart bargain.

He didn't know, though, that the rabbits had belonged to Mr. Joaquim and that they always raced to his house. The man walked away with the two animals, thinking "With the help of these rabbits, I am going to catch the thief that robbed me last week. I am going to recover all my gold. This is an investment that will easily pay for itself. Whatever I have paid for the rabbits will be nothing compared to the riches they will bring me back." He was very excited.

"My little friends," he said, "go and fetch me the thief." And he let the two rabbits run loose. They dashed away like crazy. They never came back.

By this time, Malasartes was far away. The man was furious, realizing he had been fooled. He got on his horse and went after Malasartes, who ran as fast as he could. But it was no use. The man's horse was much faster. Still running, Malasartes crossed a brook where a woman was washing her clothes. He knew he would be caught any minute.

Quick as lightning, he grabbed a poor sheep that was grazing close by and cut its belly with a knife. He pulled out the tripe and hid it inside his shirt. Then he started telling the washerwoman a long story.

"A mean farmer is after me. He wants to kill me. I am exhausted, almost all my strength is gone. There is one thing left for me to do!" said he. He made a dramatic gesture, grabbed the knife, and pretended he was cutting open his own belly. He produced the sheep's tripe and let it fall on the floor. He sighed.

"Well, I am much lighter now. Without my guts, I can run much faster. Good-bye, lady," he said as he hurried away.

The washerwoman was almost in shock after witnessing such a terrible scene. That was when the mean farmer appeared and asked if she had seen a young man running away.

"For sure! He talked to me, then all of sudden he grabbed his knife and cut his own belly. He discarded his own guts and said that he felt much lighter and quicker this way."

"So he wants to fool me again!" said the man. "But he won't. I will show him. I am going to do the same thing and run as much as he does." He grabbed the knife and cut his own belly. And of course, he died right away.

And Malasartes was free from one more of his persecutors.

PART 6

SCARY TALES

*T*his part includes a variety of strange tales of the supernatural. Those about skulls and devils probably come from European traditions. The tales of the Kibungo are likely of African origin. And the weird Creature of Fire may come from Native Brazilian lore.

The chants in some of these tales serve to create suspense. It is fun to repeat these chants in a scary voice when telling the story. Some were probably sung at one time, so you could even create a spooky tune to sing them.

THE SKULL TAKES REVENGE

*P*edro liked to make fun of everybody. He was full of jokes and always ready to tell a tall tale. Every evening he met his friends to chat and drink beer. And as the chat was always good and the beer was always icy cold, he usually came back home drunk. That was the time when he would start to pick on anyone who was around him. Very often he would start a fight. Soon, nobody wanted to escort him home, for there was always trouble on the way.

"Which one of us is the strongest?" Pedro would ask anyone who ventured near him.

Very often he would make fun of older or weaker folks. As nobody ever dared to answer back, Pedro became worse and worse. One evening as he went home, Pedro decided to take a shortcut through the cemetery. While he was wandering around the graveyard, he found a tall tree and realized that there was a skull stuck in one of the branches. The rest of the skeleton was on the ground.

"I wonder what kind of fruit is this!" he exclaimed. He pulled the poor skull from the branch and examined it. The skull, with all its white teeth showing, seemed to be smiling at him. Pedro burst into laughter.

"I see you are just like me, a good-natured guy, always smiling at everybody," he said. Then he added. "Since we have so much in common, I would like to invite you to have supper at my home, tomorrow at midnight. Don't fail to show up! I am sure my friends will be dying to meet you! It will be a riot!"

Then, he let the skull fall to the ground and kicked it as if it were a soccer ball. He was still laughing as he got home and dropped into bed and fell fast asleep.

On the next day, he woke up with a terrible headache. He was feeling so bad that he decided to go to his neighbor's house and ask him to make some tea. His friend stared at him, and then told him angrily.

"No more jokes, Pedro. Don't ask anything else from me again. How can you say that you are feeling sick if you keep this horrible grin on your face? You must stop making fun of everybody, Pedro!" And the neighbor slammed the door.

Pedro didn't understand his neighbor's reaction. He wasn't even trying to be funny. He was too sick for that. He stumbled back into his own kitchen and managed to make some tea. As he started drinking, something even stranger happened. The hot liquid started dripping from the corners of his mouth, as if it were open without his knowledge. Pedro ran to the nearest mirror. He froze when he gazed at his own reflection. His mouth was wide open, his teeth flashing in the daylight, frozen in a hideous grin. Pedro didn't feel like grinning at all, but he couldn't help it.

It didn't take long for Pedro to recover from the fright. He wasn't the kind of guy who worried too long about anything.

"Better be laughing than crying," he thought. Pedro went back to the kitchen to fix dinner for his guests. He set the table for thirteen guests. He didn't remember that on the night before he had invited one more, while roaming drunk around the graveyard.

Around midnight, his guests started to knock on the door. They entered and sat at the table. When all the seats were taken, Pedro started pouring the wine. When the clock struck midnight, he heard somebody else knocking on the door. A darkened shape stood outside, all wrapped in a long cloak that covered the stranger from head to toe.

"I hope you haven't forgotten me, my friend. I have decided to accept your kind invitation and come to dinner."

That was when Pedro remembered the skull and his jokes at the cemetery, the night before. Trembling with fear, but keeping the hideous grin on his face, Pedro offered the mysterious guest his own seat and poured him a glass of wine.

Suddenly, the guest let the cloak fall over his shoulders and raised his glass, offering a toast. There was no face to be seen, just a smiling skull. Pedro's friends leapt up, screaming. Pedro himself tried to get up, but ended by dropping heavily on the floor.

"Isn't that funny," shouted the skull, "the man who had no fear now faints in terror." And the creature got up from the table and left the house with slow and heavy footsteps.

Some of Pedro's friends tried to help him. But there was nothing that they could do. He lay there with that ghastly grin on his face. But Pedro had not fainted. Pedro was dead. Dead of fright.

THE DEVIL IN A BOTTLE

*O*nce upon a time there was a man who was so jealous of his wife that he would not leave her by herself for a minute. The woman was young, beautiful, and sociable. She loved to go to parties and enjoy the company of her numerous friends. Her husband did not like that at all. All he wanted was for her to stay home, cooking and sewing for him and doing her wifely duties, as he would often tell her. They would only go to dances if she promised not to talk to anyone. And if anyone looked at her, waved, or smiled, the husband would get so upset that he would drag her back home immediately. The woman could not stand her husband's jealousy anymore.

One day, the man had to go on a business trip. The thought of leaving his wife alone was torturing him. He could not even sleep at night. He spent his days grumbling about the situation and trying to think of a solution. On the evening before the trip, tired from thinking so hard about the problem, he started cursing. "I don't know what else to do. Only the Devil himself would be able to help me!" he yelled.

There was the roar of thunder; a fetid smoke filled the room and a figure covered in shadows appeared in front of him. It was the Devil.

"Why did you invoke my name? What do you want from me? Be quick, because I have plenty to do," said the Devil, a bit upset at being called at such a late time.

Very pale, the man realized that he could not send the Devil away with no explanations. He decided to ask him for something.

"The problem is that I must travel tomorrow morning, and I would like to ask you to take care of my wife for a few days."

The Devil smiled and accepted the task immediately.

"This is going to be a piece of cake. And I will probably get another lost soul in the bargain," he thought.

The man thanked the Devil profusely and felt relieved. He was sure that he could not leave his wife in better hands.

Before leaving home on the next day, the man said farewell to his wife.

"My darling, I want you to get some rest while I am gone. So I have hired a young man as a servant to help you do all your daily tasks. He has been instructed to do everything you ask him to do. He has wonderful recommendations. Therefore, relax and get some rest while I am gone." And then he left.

The woman decided to test the new servant right away. She started giving him orders. "Go cut all the wood that is in the backyard," she said. Before she went back to the kitchen, the Devil had already finished the task.

"Go pick up all the fruit in our orchard." She had just to turn her back and the Devil was bringing all the fruit to her.

Soon the woman started getting tired of the employee, who never left her side for a single moment. It didn't matter how absurd the task was . . . in a few moments it was done and he was back at her side.

"This is so strange. I think my husband left the Devil himself to look after me," she thought. Then she had an idea. She devised a very special task to entertain the servant from hell.

"I would like you to go to the river and bring water enough to fill these two pits," she told him the next morning. And then she gave him a sieve! The Devil started to work. He would go to the river, which was a mile away, fill the sieve with water, and run to the house, only to the discover that the container was empty again. Then he would start the work all over again. And that was how he spent the day, running back and forth. It was all that the woman wanted. She spent the day away, talking to her friends, visiting in the village, and doing everything her husband usually forbade her to do. When she came back home, it was already dark. She found the Devil lying on the floor, completely exhausted. But she was no fool, and she decided to have a conversation with the special servant.

"I am truly impressed by your service. You are so accomplished that sometimes it looks like a miracle. I have made you work so much that I really hesitate to ask you to do one more thing. Please tell me if this is too hard for you, all right?" said the woman with her sweetest and most innocent air.

The Devil was so proud of all the praise that he told her he would do anything she asked.

"You seem to be able to do such incredible feats. Would you be able to get inside this bottle to recover my ring that fell inside? I know this is almost impossible and I doubt that you can do it," said the woman, provoking the Devil.

She didn't even have to ask twice. Proud of himself, the Devil wanted to show her the extent of his power. So he quickly got himself into the bottle. As fast as she could, the woman closed the bottle with a lid. The Devil became a prisoner of the bottle. And she got all the precious freedom she needed so much. While her guardian was imprisoned, she spent wonderful days doing exactly what she pleased.

When her husband came back, she enveloped him in hugs. His wife had never been so gentle and attentive. Soon he wanted to know where the new servant was.

"Sweetie, he left one day and never came back. I didn't miss him at all. He was like the Devil. Notice how smelly the house is. It smells like sulphur!"

And the smell was really awful. The devil was burning with wrath inside the bottle.

The man agreed. "What a stench! What are we going to do?"

The woman came up with an idea.

"Dear husband, I think you should hurry to the church with this bottle and fill it with holy water. Then we can spray it all around the house and see what happens."

The man obeyed. He went to the church, but when he removed the lid from the bottle to fill it with holy water, there was a roar of thunder. The Devil appeared, looking confused, and disappeared as fast as lightning. Nobody saw him again.

The man was so startled that when he got back home, he couldn't explain what had happened. But his wife looked so happy that he was sure that she had something to do with it. She had done something. But this was a secret she would take to the grave.

And that is why the people say:

"When a woman wants something, not even the Devil can stand in her way."

THE HEADLESS MULE

*O*nce upon a time there was a prosperous farmer who owned much land and employed many hands on his fields. He was a fair man, who treated his servers well and was beloved by all.

Once he had to leave the farm and travel to the capital, where he stayed for two months doing business. When he came back, he had news to tell. "I want to introduce my wife to you all. From now on, I hope you treat her as the queen of this land. Her wish is the law from now on."

The girl was beautiful, very gentle and sweet to everyone. Soon she had many friends around the neighborhood. She enjoyed dancing and frequently invited her friends for balls, dinners, and concerts. Life on the farm had never been so much fun. There was happiness everywhere, but no one was happier than her husband.

Then strange things started to happen. Almost every Friday morning, half-eaten animals where found in the field. There was blood everywhere.

The farm hands often missed one or two sheep, one pig or a cow.

"What a strange thing. Who did that? There must be a monster around or a ghost," people said.

"That is silly. There is certainly a hungry jaguar around the woods."

But every week, the same thing happened. Always on a Friday morning. The workers were worried and decided to relate the strange events to the farmer. He decided to take care of the matter and solve the mystery.

He anxiously waited for a week. On Thursday night, he got ready to go. He waited till midnight, got a gun, and went to the fields.

The night was dark, with no moon or stars in the sky. There was a deep silence. The farmer looked around, but he couldn't see anything different. He waited outside for hours and hours, but nothing happened. He was about to go back home when he heard noises behind the house in the shed where the sheep slept. He ran as fast as he could. As he approached the shed, he felt his blood freeze. There was something mingled with the shadows—it was too dark to distinguish—and the creature was devouring the leg of a lamb. Horrified, the farmer ran toward the monster.

He stood paralyzed, out of breath, as he realized that the creature, who was still chewing the raw meat, covered with blood, was his own wife. When she saw the farmer, she let out a horrible shriek and suddenly turned into a headless mule! Turning, the mule-with-no-head galloped away down the road.

The farmer was found by his employees the next morning. His eyes were wide open, his face was frozen with fear, and he was mute. He never recovered from the horrors of that night. And he never spoke again.

His beautiful wife had disappeared, and no one ever heard from her or had news about her. The neighbors decided that she had run away with another man and that was why the husband had become mad. But from that day on, there were stories of people who saw . . . very late on Thursday nights . . . a headless mule, running madly on the roads. To this day that running, headless mule is met charging down the road sometime after midnight on Thursdays. Those who try to approach the creature are often trampled to death by her powerful hooves.

If some brave man manages to cut the mule with his knife and cause her to bleed, the spell is ended. There appears a beautiful woman, crying, full of regrets. She doesn't become a mule ever again. And the brave young man has gained a kind and beautiful wife. But early every Friday morning, new headless mules appear to haunt the roads. Those who are forced to walk at night must just hide the whites of their eyes and close their mouths so that no white teeth show. Then, with closed eyes and clenched teeth, they must mutter softly over and over, "I don't believe in the headless mule, I don't believe in the headless mule, I don't believe in the headless mule."

CREATURE OF THE NIGHT

*M*aria lived all alone in a hut by the shore. Her life was work: waking up before sunrise, carrying heavy buckets of water from the well, drying meat in the sun. It was work all day long. Her only companion was a dog, who followed her faithfully wherever she went. Sometimes she dreamed of a better, joyful life, full of laughter and music. But the dream always faded into tedious reality.

One day, at sunset, Maria was home, when she heard a distant melody. It was so sweet that it made her want to laugh and cry at the same time. It was a man's voice, rich and deep, dark and mysterious, but at the same time vaguely familiar. But she could not understand the words.

The voice seemed to be approaching her house. Maria felt her heart thumping. She longed to be with the possessor of that voice. Through the window, she could see a dark silhouette outside, by the door. She hurried to open it. But all of sudden, her dog began to sing back. "Go away, if you look for Maria, for Maria is not here."

When Maria opened the door there was no one there. She was mad. She kicked the dog. "Stupid animal!" she screamed.

Next day, as it grew dark, Maria heard the voice again at a distance. She tied the dog in the backyard and fastened a rope around its jaws. The dog could not open its mouth. She went to sit by the window. The song was clearer and clearer.

She saw a silhouette by the door. All of sudden, the dog, through its tied jaws, began to mumble its song. "Go away if you look for Maria, for Maria is not here."

The girl was so mad at the dog that, I am sorry to say, she killed her only companion and buried it in the backyard.

The next day, she sat by the window at sunset waiting to hear that wonderful voice. It was there, getting closer and closer to her house, with the same sweet melody.

She saw the dark silhouette by the door. All of sudden, she heard the dog's voice! "Go away, if you look for Maria, for Maria is not here." It was the dead dog. Even though it was dead and buried, it still sang from its grave.

Enraged, Maria unburied the dog, made a fire, and threw the dead animal in it. The next day, she waited anxiously for the voice by her window and watched as the dark silhouette approached her door.

All of a sudden, she heard another voice. "Go away, if you look for Maria, for Maria is not here." It was the dog, or I'd better say, the ashes of the dog, that still sang.

Blind with rage, Maria gathered the ashes and went to a cliff. There she threw the ashes in the sea.

The next day, Maria bathed in perfumed water. She combed her long black hair carefully and put on her Sunday dress. She sat silently by the window, waiting for the sunset. When darkness started to descend, she heard the voice singing faintly in the distance. The sound grew louder and louder. Her heart beat fast. The voice had never sounded so sweet, so gentle, and at the same time so strong and intense.

The dark silhouette approached her door.

There was no other voice.

And the beast came in.

This story was collected in Maranhao, in the North of Brazil, in an area where the forest and the sea meet. It originally had a chant with words that mixed Portuguese expressions with Native Brazilian language.

THE OLD LADY AND
THE MONKEY

*O*nce upon a time there lived an old lady who had plenty of banana trees in her backyard. They were so plentiful that the woman prepared all kinds of sweets with the fruit, and she became heavier and heavier. Finally she was so fat that she couldn't climb up the wooden ladder to get the bananas. As she looked up at the sweet fruit, she had an idea. She would call Monkey to help. Monkey could easily climb up the banana trees and get her the bananas.

Monkey came and quickly climbed to the top of the banana tree. The old lady shouted: "Good Monkey, now you can pick the fruits and throw them here in my basket!"

But Monkey had different plans. He began to eat the best fruit and throw down the rotten and the green bananas. The old lady had not even one good banana to eat. She was furious, and prepared her revenge.

On the next day, she made a tar doll and dressed it as a girl. She even put red ribbons on the fake doll's hair. She let the doll stand by the door of her house with a basket full of ripe bananas. Soon enough Monkey showed up and asked the girl to give him a banana.

"Girl, give me a banana!"

But the tar doll would not answer. Monkey insisted. Nothing. Monkey got angry and warned. "Hey girl, give me a banana or I will slap your face."

No answer.

Monkey slapped the doll's face and got caught by the tar.

Monkey became nervous.

"Let me go, otherwise, I will slap you with my other hand."

No answer.

Monkey slapped the doll again. His other hand also got caught.

"Let me go, or I will kick you!"

No answer.

Monkey kicked the doll again. His foot got caught.

"Let me go, or I will kick you with my other foot!"

No answer.

Monkey kicked the doll again. That foot got caught also.

"Let me go, or I will whip you with my tail!"

No answer.

Monkey whipped the doll with his tail and got caught.

Now Monkey was completely stuck on the tar doll.

The old woman came out of her hiding place inside the house with a big knife.

"I will have Monkey stew for dinner!" she chortled.

And that is just what she did. She killed the Monkey and started to prepare the meat for dinner.

But a voice could be heard singing,

"Stew me gently, stew me slow. If you change your mind, let me go."

The old lady ignored the singing voice. She put spices, vegetables, and chopped monkey into a pan and began to cook her stew. Then she heard:

"Cook me gently, cook me slow. If you change your mind, let me go."

When the stew was ready, the old lady sat down and ate with great appetite. While she ate, she could still hear a voice singing:

"Eat me gently, eat me slow. If you change your mind, let me go."

After that feast, the old lady felt really sleepy. She decided to take a siesta. She woke soon, feeling really sick. Her belly was swollen as if she were pregnant. And inside her stomach a voice was singing:

"Digest me gently. Digest me slow. Listen to me! You'd better let me go!"

"All right! All right! GO!"

Then the old lady's belly started swelling. It got bigger and bigger and bigger . . . .

Suddenly . . . it exploded!

Out flew dozens of little monkeys, who all jumped around singing, dancing, and making faces at the old woman.

"One monkey cooked gently, one monkey cooked slow . . . makes many many monkeys! Goodbye! We've got to go!"

THE CREATURE OF FIRE

*O*nce upon a time there lived a man who didn't like to share anything with others. He used to keep the doors and windows of his home closed so nobody would ask for food or shelter for the night.

Once he bought a lamb to roast and eat with his family. As he didn't want to give a single piece to his neighbors, he decided that he was going to roast the lamb in some distant, deserted place where no one could see him. He wanted a place where there were no fleas or flies, of course. Early in the morning, when it was still dark, he got the horse carriage ready and ordered that his wife and children bring the lamb. They went in search of a place without flies or mosquitoes. They drove the whole day long, going deeper and deeper into the woods. When it was getting dark, they found a large spot with no trees. The place was silent and deserted. There were no fleas or flies, or anything else.

The family climbed down from the carriage. But as soon as they started to prepare the meat to be roasted, they realized that they had not brought anything to make fire with, no embers, no coal. The woman suggested that they stop at some house and ask for help. But they were in a very deserted place, and it was getting darker and darker. When night fell, suddenly the man noticed two tiny lights shining in the distance. So he told his eldest son: "My child, go there and ask for some embers to start our fire." The boy was scared. He walked in the darkness, afraid of stepping on a snake or falling into a hole. He tried to concentrate on the distant lights. Suddenly he was blinded by a strong light. When his eyes became used to it, he realized that he was right in front of a huge creature, with fiery eyes, hairy ears, and large yellow teeth. The boy almost fainted. But there was no time for fear. The monster was getting closer, and the only thing to do was run as fast as he could to warn his family of the danger. And that was exactly what he did.

The creature let out a roar, flapped his large ears, making a horrible noise, and started to run clumsily after the boy, shouting at him:

"If you don't give me what I want, I will burn you. If you don't give me what I want, I will burn you!"

The boy ran as fast as he could, and made it to the place where his family was waiting. He could barely speak.

"Mom, Dad, let's hurry away from here. There is a creature spilling fire through his eyes. The creature is desperate. He wants us for dinner!"

The man ordered them to leave everything behind. He held his youngest son, and told his family to run as fast as they could. Right behind them, they could hear the creature with the fiery eyes screaming.

"If you don't give me what I want, I will burn you! If you don't give me what I want, I will burn you!"

They ran all through the night without stopping, because they could find no shelter, no hiding place in the woods. They were exhausted, and the creature seemed to be getting closer and closer. It was then that they passed by a small hut. Sitting on the porch was a woodsman, rolling his tobacco.

"Where are you going in such a hurry in the dead of night?" asked the man.

"Woodsman, it is something awful! There is a huge monster running after us. He claims that he wants to devour all of us"

"Come on in and hide. Let me take care of him personally!"

The woodsman got his shotgun ready and sat again on the porch. He kept rolling his handmade cigarettes.

Soon enough, the monster with fiery eyes appeared, running on the road. The woodsman held his gun and concentrated.

"If you don't give me what I want, I will burn you. If you don't give me what I want, I will burn you!"

The monster approached the woodsman and asked if he had seen a man, a woman, and two children. The woodsman didn't answer, and kept on doing what he had been doing before. The monster repeated the question, enraged at the time the man was taking to answer.

"If you don't give me what I want, I will burn you. If you don't give me what I want, I will burn you."

And he was about to step into the house when the woodsman took aim and . . . pop. He hit the monster in the legs. The creature fell on the floor, letting out a terrible yell. The woodsman called the man and asked for his help. They both hit the monster with sticks and stones, till it lay lifeless on the floor. Then they dragged the creature of fire far away, where only the buzzards would keep him company.

Once he was rested and recovered from the fright, the man told the whole story to the woodsman. The woodsman gave him some good advice.

"My friend, never look for a place with no fleas or flies. Fleas or flies are a bother. But monsters are much worse."

The man and his family went back home the next day. And to show that he had changed his ways, the man had an ox killed and called all the neighbors to share the meat with them. Now he welcomes travelers into his home. And he always tells them the story of the creature of fire . . . the creature that lurked in a place where there were no fleas and no flies.

THE BEETLE MAN

*O*nce upon a time there lived a girl who wanted to marry someone really special. She had many suitors, but she found faults in each of them. Some were not rich enough. Some were not good looking enough.

One day she was standing by the window when she saw a very handsome young man, dressed in the finest clothes she had ever seen. She called her father immediately and said:

"Do you see that man over there? That is the one I want to marry."

"But my dear, you have refused so many worthy young men who have knocked on our door. And now, you decide that you want to get married to someone you don't even know!"

But there was no use trying to call the girl to her senses. She had already made up her mind. Her father called the young man in, and after awhile the young man asked the girl to marry him.

There was a huge wedding party, and the girl was very happy with her husband, who seemed to be as special as she had always fancied.

After the wedding, they went to live on a farm, far away from the village. And the girl was very happy for a while. What she didn't know was that while she slept every night, the young man changed into a giant beetle. He used to fly into the corral, choose an animal, and drink all its blood. Then he would change into human shape again and would go back to bed as if nothing had happened.

The girl had no idea of her husband's night activities. She tried to please him as much as possible. She prepared his favorite food, washed his clothes carefully, and took loving care of their home. When night came, she was so tired that she never awoke when her husband left their bed.

But time went by, and the young man changed. He spent most of the day away and he complained about all she did. The girl became frightened of the man she had married. Finally, one night she woke up in the darkness and found that her husband was not in bed. He only came back after sunrise, scowling. When she asked where he had been, he just said he had been out for a walk.

One day, the girl decided to stay up the whole night, to try to discover where her husband went. When the rooster sang the first time, her husband rose from bed carefully and tiptoed out of the room. She followed him silently. The young man opened the door, and

---

when he got into the yard, he started shaking all over. He turned into a giant black beetle and flew away.

The poor girl saw the beetle fly toward the corral and then bleed the last sheep they had and drink its blood. By then, he had already killed all the animals they had, cow, horse, pig, and lambs. The girl was frozen with fear, knowing now why her husband left their bed every night. "This is what he does! It doesn't look good at all!"

Later that day, the girl said:

"My dear, my father sent me a message. It seems that my mother is very sick. I would like to go home"

"You can go. But you should leave your parents' home when the rooster sings for the first time. When the rooster sings for the second time, you should be halfway home. And when the rooster sings for the third time, you must be back here!"

The girl went to visit her parents and told them the whole story. Her folks were desolate.

"You chose among so many suitors and none was good enough for you. You ended up getting married to a man who turns into a beast. You have nothing to do but to put up with this."

In the evening, as soon as the rooster sang for the first time, she left her parents' home. When it sang for the second time, she was halfway there, and when it sang for the third time, she was back home with her husband. She kept living with him, but she was frightened all the time.

As he had already killed all the animals on the farm, the man was in a horrible mood, because he had no more blood to drink. He didn't spare even the chickens. One night, he sat on the bed and started singing.

"I feel thirsty.

I want to drink.

Blood, blood, blood.

I want to drink blood!"

The girl awoke in a panic.

"I have to go away! Now that there is no animal left, he will come for my blood!"

As soon as her husband went out that night, she gathered all her belongings and ran away to her parents' home. When the husband came back and realized that she had left, he was furious, because he was really planning to kill her that night.

From that day on, he would go every night in his beetle shape to visit the garden of his father in law, where he would kiss the flowers and buzz:

"I feel thirsty.

I want to drink.

Blood, blood, blood.

I want to drink blood!"

He was hoping to see the girl and take her by force. But the girl was no fool. She never gave him the chance. After a long time, he flew away and never came back. The girl never heard from her husband again.

The Kibungo

The Kibungo is the frequent protagonist of many tales of oral literature in Bahia state, located in the Northeast of Brazil. This ogre has an opening in the middle of his back. The opening gets bigger when he bends his head forward and closes when he raises his head again. His stomach is there, and it is there that he puts children and women, whom he eats without swallowing. And it is through this hole that his victims sometimes are rescued, still alive. He can be killed by stabbing, shooting, or severe beating. He is bad, always hungry, treacherous, and cowardly. This character appears in African-influenced tales from Bahia. He appears in tales with happy or tragic endings, but always in some distant, vague location. He perpetually threatens children, and like the boogeyman, he is used as a means to discipline. In most of the Kibungo stories we find rhymes and music, which show their relation to stories sung and told in Africa. The Kibungo stories were brought to Brazil by the Bantu slaves. The slaves were taken all over the country, but the Kibungo stories remained strictly in Bahia.

THE GIRL AND THE KIBUNGO

*A*long time ago, when the nights were much darker than nowadays, the children could not go out to play by themselves. There was a kibungo in the neighborhood. He could be heard moaning, "Hum, hum, hum!" When he found a child, he would grab the poor child and would have him or her for dinner.

In this place, there was a woman who had only one daughter. The girl liked to go out in the evenings, visiting the neighbors and her relatives, who lived nearby. Her mother would get worried.

"My dear, don't do this. You should not leave the house in the evening. The kibungo is outside, and he may catch you and eat you!"

But the girl was very stubborn, and she wouldn't pay any attention to what her poor mother said.

One very dark night when the girl was walking down the street she felt a warm breath on her neck and heard dragging footsteps really close. Completely frightened, she tried to run, but it was already too late. The kibungo caught her, put her inside his back, and went away ready to eat her. The girl started crying. When she passed by her mother's house, she started singing:

"Mummy dearest,

Kibungo terere

Who I love from my heart,

Kibungo terere

Help me, please.

Kibungo terere

Kibungo wants to eat me."

The mother answered:

"I told you so.

Kibungo terere

That you should not be out at night.

Kibungo terere

When she heard that, the girl cried even more and started calling for her friends and relatives. But no one wanted to help her, and every one answered the same way. She kept crying in the hole in the back of the kibungo. She went by the house of many relatives, but they were all scared and no one tried to help her.

It was then that her grandmother noticed the noises in the street and saw people running and screaming. The old lady stood by the window to watch what was happening.

"The Kibungo caught your granddaughter. He is coming with the girl in his back!"

The old lady didn't think twice. She went running to the kitchen and put some water to boil and put an iron skewer over the embers.

When the kibungo got closer to her grandmother's house, the girl sang:

"Granny dearest,

Kibungo terere

That I love with all my heart,

Kibungo terere

Help me, please.

Kibungo terere

Kibungo wants to eat me."

The grandmother answered just like the others, and the kibungo, very full of himself, strolled by the house carelessly. When he was right under the window, the grandmother poured all the boiling water on his legs. Filled with pain, the kibungo jerked his body and threw the girl out on the ground. The old woman grabbed the iron skewer, which was hot from the fire, and pierced his neck. Although he was wounded, the kibungo still managed to run away, screaming and bawling.

The grandmother came to help her granddaughter, and she let her stay in her house until she had recovered from the fright. From that day on, the girl didn't want to wander around in the evenings.

The kibungo was seriously wounded, and he disappeared for a long time. But everybody knew that he was still alive and that, when everybody least expected, he would be back to catch careless children in the dark of the night.

THE KIBUNGO AND THE BOY WITH THE SACK FULL OF FEATHERS

*O*nce upon a time there was a boy who liked to go to the woods to hunt for birds. He was very clever. He never did the birds any harm. He would talk to them, give them ripe fruit, and then he let them fly away. From each bird, he would get two feathers, which he kept in a bag. Day after day, the bag became more and more filled with colorful feathers. His parents had no idea why he wanted so many feathers.

"Dear son, what do you intend to do with so many feathers?" they asked. "These feathers are good for nothing."

"Mother, father, please don't ask me any questions right now, because I can't answer. The feathers will be necessary when the time comes," he answered coolly.

When summer came, the whole family left for a fishing trip by a river far away from their home. It was going to be a long journey, and the preparations began several days before. The women cooked the food, the young ones fixed the nets and the straw baskets, and the older men examined the fishing rods and the bait. But the boy stayed quiet in his corner, watching everything, doing nothing.

On the next morning, very early, he grabbed his bag full of feathers and prepared to leave with the others.

His father was puzzled. "You are not going to take this with you, son! Let this bag stay at home and help me with the baskets."

"I have to bring the bag with me. Don't worry. I am strong and I can carry the bag and the baskets, too," said the boy, who was actually thin and small for his age. To his father's surprise, he kept his word and carried the bag and the baskets.

When they arrived at the fishing spot, the women lit the fire and started heating the food. The men gathered the fishing rods and went into the river, talking lively. Just the boy remained alone on the bank of the river, holding his bag, and looking closely at the other men.

They had been in the river for hours and had no luck so far. The fish didn't even bite their bait. There was no sign of fish, not even the smallest ones.

"My folks, beware," said one of the fishermen, "there must be a Kibungo here."

"Are you crazy? There is no such a thing as a Kibungo. Soon the fish will come back," answered those who didn't believe that there was such a creature in the woods.

And they kept the argument going for awhile, then suddenly they heard a terrible snort coming from the heart of the woods, far away. They were all paralyzed with fear. Then the shouting started, and they were running in all directions, screaming.

"It is the Kibungo! Run for your lives!"

"I told you so. You didn't believe me. And now he is here!"

"What is going to happen to us now? What about the children? We have to run away!"

"There will not be enough time for us to get back home. Everything is lost! We are going to be eaten by the Kibungo!"

When everybody seemed to be ready to flee, the boy spoke.

"Don't run. Wait. Keep calm and quiet. Stand in line and listen carefully to what I have to say." The folks were so scared that they did what he told them and stood in line. The boy then gave to each a feather of the wing and a feather of the tail of a bird. And he recommended that they keep the wing feather between their teeth and the tail feather under their armpits.

When he had finished distributing the feathers, the boy emptied the sack on the floor, and there were two last feathers left there, for him. He took the last spot in line and told everyone to keep their wits and stay as calm as possible.

Again, they heard that terrible snort, much closer. The Kibungo was right there, huge, frightening, snorting, and smashing the twigs. He approached the first in line and was already reaching for him, when the boy, at the end of the line started to sing:

"This is my father, Aue,

Gangarue, fall,

Don't fall."

The Kibungo let out a yell and took away his hand from the man. He went to the second person in line. The boy sang:

"This is my mother, Aue,

Gangarue, fall,

Don't fall."

The Kibungo let out another scream and shrank away from the woman. And he went to all the relatives of the boy, brothers, grandparents, uncles, aunts, and cousins. He couldn't get a single one of them for a snack because every time he stretched his claws, the boy sang the same song.

As the Kibungo advanced, wings started to appear on the people he left behind. When the boy's turn came, he put one wing between his teeth and the second one under his armpits, and he also got wings. Under the boy's instructions, all started flapping their wings and took off, flying high and leaving the Kibungo behind. One by one they all got back home, still amazed by all that had happened and still scared. They sat and talked.

"Now we are safe. The Kibungo will not come here. We should all go to sleep because tomorrow is another day," said one of the men.

"No, you are wrong. The Kibungo will come. We have to find a way to keep him away for good," said the worried boy. Soon he had an idea.

"I know what we should do. We should dig a deep pit right in front of the door. Then we put in the bottom of the pit very sharp sticks, all pointing up. Then we have to cover everything with banana tree leaves and mud, so the Kibungo will not notice the pit. Then we put a doll sitting in a chair, just like us, and we leave it sitting next to the pit. When the Kibungo comes, he will think the doll is one of our family and will attack it. He will fall into the pit and will be pierced by the sharp sticks. This time, he won't escape!"

And that was exactly what they did. While some dug the pit, others cut the sticks and prepared the doll, dressing it with old clothes and even a straw hat. Everybody helped, and they soon finished the trap. Everything was perfect, and they hid themselves.

It was a great thing that they had been so fast. The snorts started very soon, and the Kibungo approached. Finally he saw the doll sitting by the door. He showed his long teeth, snorted some more, and jumped. But when he stepped on the banana leaves, they sank, and he fell into the pit and was pierced by the sharp sticks. He died immediately.

Everybody ran to see the dead Kibungo, and they were overjoyed. They sang and danced, and started a big celebration. The house was full of laughter and music. They were free now, free from the terrible Kibungo, and now they could go fishing whenever they chose to, without fear.

The boy was acknowledged as the hero of the day and was praised for his wisdom, for knowing how to escape from the monster and then showing how to vanquish him. His parents were proud and surprised at their child's qualities, and they never stopped repeating:

"What an incredible son we have. He vanquished a terrible Kibungo using just a sack full of feathers."

The boy would listen to them, smiling and saying nothing.

PART 7

DEATH TALES IN BRAZIL

$\mathcal{M}$any tales in Brazil deal with attempts at cheating Death. They are usually funny stories that express the wish to see Death delayed as much as possible. The hero uses tricks, traps, and disguises to achieve this feat, but in the end, Death always wins. Even in the magical universe of folktales, Death certainly has the last word. In Brazilian tradition Death is portrayed as an old woman in black. The word for Death is feminine in Spanish and Portuguese, hence Death is a lady.

HOW THE BLACKSMITH FOOLED DEATH

*O*nce upon a time, there was a young man who worked as a blacksmith in a small town. Though he worked hard every single day, he had barely enough to buy food for himself and his wife.

One day, when he was running errands in a neighboring town, he found an old lady sitting by the road, looking too weak to go on her way.

"Excuse me, young man," said the woman feebly, "I have been without food for three days. Please give me something to eat, it can be a piece of old bread, because I am almost starving to death."

The blacksmith had a good heart. He opened his sack and found a bit of bread and lean meat. In fact, that was all they would have to eat at his home. But he was young and strong, and he could certainly bear a day without food. The old woman swallowed the food rapidly, thanking him. Then, feeling stronger, she started to talk. She told him she knew about his life, his work, and his good heart. She had magical powers and she would like to reward him for his kindness.

"You can make three wishes, and they will come true," said the old lady.

After much thinking, the blacksmith spoke firmly:

"I want iron and coal enough to be able to work without worries for the rest of my life. I want a magical table that will always be covered with food when I or my wife are hungry. And I want a magical guitar, that when played by me, makes people dance without being able to stop."

"You deserve everything, my friend," said the woman as she disappeared from sight.

From that day on, the life of the blacksmith changed dramatically. He always had iron and coal handy. This way he was able to produce more and not get as tired. Well fed, he and his wife lived happily. Time went by, and the blacksmith aged without noticing.

One day, someone knocked at his door. It was Death.

"I came to take you, Mr. Blacksmith. The time of your easy life is done."

The man invited Death in, but when the wife saw that dark, frightening figure there in the living room, announcing that she had come to take her husband, the woman could not help but start crying:

"Don't take my dear husband, my lady. He still has many years to spend by my side," she begged.

"His time has come. There is nothing I can do about it."

The blacksmith asked his sobbing wife to leave the room, explaining that he needed to do some private talking with Death.

"I understand that my time is done. I will go in peace, but before that, I think I have the right to a last wish. I would like to play the guitar for the last time." Death agreed, but asked him to be fast, because she had many others to visit that day. She was one busy lady.

The old blacksmith got the guitar from the closet. He sat on a comfortable chair and started to play. Immediately, Death started shaking. She jumped and she started dancing around the living room. "Stop that!" she screamed, with fear in her voice.

"I won't!" said the blacksmith, laughing and playing. "Paro nada!" "Not for anything!" He laughed fiercely and kept on playing. Death was shaking her hips, waving her arms, and tap dancing. She was getting tired. With a weak voice, she begged the blacksmith to stop playing.

"I will only stop if you give me three more years to live. I have plenty to do."

"It is too much. You are already too old!" said Death, completely exhausted.

The blacksmith kept on playing.

"I need at least two more years. I want to travel and to make new friends. I am still full of energies!"

"I can't do this," said Death, breathless, "I have a task to accomplish!"

The old man started playing even faster. Death barely touched the living room floor, but she still refused to strike a deal. The blacksmith insisted.

"Either you give me two more years, or I will still be playing at the end of time."

After much talk, Death was so exhausted that she agreed to come back in two years to take him.

And life went on. In two years, the blacksmith did everything he wanted. He traveled, he worked, he made new friends. But when you are happy, time goes by fast. He barely noticed that the day of the new visit of Death was getting closer and closer.

One afternoon, someone knocked at the door. The blacksmith's wife opened it and found Death standing there, with a wary look.

"I came to take your husband away. His time is over."

Luckily, the blacksmith had gone out, and his wife didn't know when he would be back. Death was very displeased.

"Tell him that I will come back in a week. He'd better be here waiting for me!"

When the blacksmith returned, he found his wife crying. She told him everything. He had an idea. He darkened his hair. He put on a fake beard, fake moustache, and sunglasses. One week later, at the appointed day, they turned off the lights in the living room, leaving only the candles lit. When Death knocked at the door, the woman opened it and said.

"It is a pity you took so long to get here, Madam Death. My husband waited for you the whole day, but he had to leave. It was an emergency, you know, a matter of life or death. Maybe it would be a good idea if you went looking for him. Who knows, you might find him on the road?"

Death became very angry.

"Your husband is a liar! He is trying to cheat me again. This is not fair. We had a deal!"

Death started to walk around the house. When she entered the kitchen, she found the man.

"I see you have visitors," she said, trying hard to examine the man with beard and glasses. The house was really dark.

"This is my uncle," lied the woman. "He came in for a visit."

Death was in a hurry, as always. She looked around thoughtfully. The she spoke:

"Well, today I have to do my task. Since your husband is not here, I will be taking your uncle in his stead."

And the old blacksmith, who had fooled Death twice, ended his days among the living.

THE GOOD MINISTER
AND DEATH

*O*nce upon a time, in a faraway country, there lived a very powerful king, who ruled his country with a fair hand.

One of his ministers was more obedient and faithful than all the others.

Every day, he would go to the throne room to greet the king. When he realized that the monarch was in a good mood, this minister would beg to be nominated governor of a distant town. He would justify his plea with any excuses he could come up with.

But the king didn't want to see his favorite minister leaving the court. He would always give him the same answer: "NO!"

The poor man would take the sovereign's answer humbly. He waited for time to go by, so the king would forget, and he would go back and again make his request. But the answer was always the same: "NO! NO! NO!"

After many years of this, the king was getting tired of the insistence of the minister.

His faithful server decided to explain the real reason behind his wish to leave the court. He told the king that every day, as he left his room, he met Death by his door, staring at him, wide eyed. He couldn't stand that terrible sight anymore. He was going crazy.

The king listened to this patiently. But he didn't believe a single word that the old man said. The poor man was becoming senile, he thought. It was a pity, but he could not trust his judgment anymore. He felt sorry for him and decided to send him to the place he longed to be.

Weeks later, while he was walking around the gardens of the palace, the king met Death. He decided to begin a conversation.

"Why are you chasing my old minister, madam Death? He told me you were always staring at him, wide eyed as if you were surprised."

Death answered:

"It is simple, your majesty. A while ago, I had received orders to meet him in a village where he had been appointed governor. I should go there and take him with me. But time went by, and he never went there. Every morning, as he left his room, I was surprised to see that he was still around here. It took me a long time, but I finally accomplished my task."

Days later, the king received the news of the death of his most loyal minister.

AUNT MISERY'S
PEAR TREE

*M*isery was an old lady, who had to beg to live. She was already very old, and to live she relied only on what the goodwill of others would give her and on the pears from the tall pear tree that stood in her yard. But for the last few years, it had been harder and harder for her to pick the fruits. The children in the neighborhood would climb the tree and eat the best fruit. Old Misery had only the rotten ones left to eat.

One stormy evening, a poor man knocked on her door. He was starving, seemed to be very weak, and needed food and a place to rest. Misery had little to offer, but she made him a bowl of hot soup, gave him some bread, and let him eat whatever he wanted. She gave him her own bed, with plenty of blankets, and she went to sleep on the floor, by the fire.

The next morning, the man woke up feeling better and started to get ready to leave. Misery even insisted that he drink a cup of coffee and gave him the last bit of bread in the house. As he was leaving, the man thanked her and said that he would be able to grant her a wish. Anything she wanted.

"I have power, and I will give you what you need."

Misery was so used to having little, she didn't even know what to ask. She had to think for a long time.

"There is one thing that makes me mad. I hate to see people climbing the tree and eating all my pears. I wish those who climbed the pear tree, without my permission, would stay stuck there till I gave them permission to climb down."

The man left after assuring her that her wish was granted.

On that same day, Misery discovered that he had told the truth. The kids who climbed her pear tree were stuck at the top of the tree, and could only climb down after being hit by the old woman with a stick and bitten by her dog, too. Soon enough, no one else dared to get near the tree. The old woman was able to enjoy all the fruit by herself.

Many years went by. Misery became stronger. She was well fed from eating all those pears.

One day, someone knocked on her door. It was a tall and lean woman, dressed in black, bearing a sickle.

"Follow me, Misery. Your time has come!"

The old woman recognized Death, but she had no intention of following her. She still felt strong and full of life. She thought for a while, and then she said to the visitor:

"Madam, I agree that I should follow you. But before I go, I think I have the right to have a last wish. I would appreciate if I could eat one of the fruits of my beautiful pear tree. But as you know, I am too old to climb it now. I would beg you to go there and to bring me those four last pears."

Death agreed, and started to climb the tree with impressive speed. She got the fruits, but when it was time to climb down, she got stuck among the branches. She begged Misery to free her. It was no use. Misery would not allow her to come down. Misery was happy. As long as Death stayed in the tree, Misery could go on living for many years.

And many years went by. But Death started to be missed in the world. The hospitals were full of sick people, because no one would die. There were people who were almost 200 years old who would try everything to die: they threw themselves off cliffs, they stopped eating, but even then they would not die. The gravediggers, the coffin manufacturers, and the people who prayed for the dead had no work to do and lived in penury. They were all calling for Death and asking her to come to take those people away.

One day, a gravedigger who had become a close friend to Death went by Misery's house and saw his friend at the top of the tree. He climbed the tree immediately, to try to help her, but he also got stuck.

When the situation seemed to be getting out of control, Misery decided to heed the pleas of the people and let Death climb down the tree. But she asked one thing first. Death would never dare come to take her again.

Death accepted Misery's condition. She climbed down the tree and took anyone who crossed her path. Thousands of people died, but finally order was reestablished in the world.

Death kept her word. And that is why Misery is alive around the world today.

PART 8

FESTIVAL GAMES AND RECIPES FROM BRAZIL

BRAZILIAN FESTIVALS

*B*razil is a Catholic country. Many of the festivities during the year are celebrations to honor the saints. Although some of the most traditional festivals take place in the countryside, the June festivals honoring Saint Anthony (June 13), Saint John (June 24), and Saint Peter (June 29) are still very popular all around the country. These are also harvest festivals. Boys and girls wear special clothes that reproduce the way peasants of the olden days used to dress for their parties. The boys wear checkered shirts and jeans with colorful patches that pretend to be covering holes, and they usually draw fake beards and moustaches on their faces. Girls wear colorful dresses in flowery fabrics, adorned with lace and ribbons. They put pigtails and ribbons in their hair, and this is the one time of the year that they are allowed to use makeup. Sometimes they also paint dimples on their faces.

Boys and girls do dances that are vaguely similar to the European court dances of the early nineteenth century, so some of the commands are mispronunciations of French words. They are not very different from American square dances. A master of ceremonies announces what is going to come next. The dancers might jump when he announces there is a snake on the way; duck to protect themselves from the rain; or form a tunnel, through which each couple passes. The music comes from the concertina, with lots of percussion to set the pace.

The June festivals were originally harvest celebrations held to honor the three most popular Catholic saints: Saint Anthony, the matchmaker (June 13); Saint John (June 24); and Saint Peter (June 29). The festivals are pretty big all over Brazil. In Bahia, in the Northeast, they even determine the school year. The first term finishes before Saint John's day, because no students have their minds on studies once the festival season approaches. In the Southeast the first term usually runs into the first week of July. Sometimes the festival is organized at the churchyard, but anyone can organize them. Schools keep them in their calendar, and the students usually rehearse for weeks before the dances. There are lots of games, including the typical carnival games ball toss, pin the tail on the donkey, and fish pond. There is also dancing and food, especially all sorts of corn dishes . . . even corn dogs!

Festival Game

This is a party game played during the June festivals. Traditionally, the rhythm is established by a concertina player. There is a story that goes with this game/dance. A bride is surrounded by her parents. The bridegroom wants to run away. Her parents call the sheriff and his helpers, who bring the straying bridegroom back to the church, where the priest is waiting. He celebrates the wedding and then everybody parties. This story is enacted in Brazil from kindergarten on. Even the older kids seem to get a kick out of the story.

We Are Going to the June Festival (Quadrilha)

We are going to the party, it is a long way to the arraial (party site). So we must do everything that the master says.

Master:

> *Girls stand on one side, forming a line.*
>
> *Boys stand on the opposite side, each boy facing a girl.*

(They line up.)

Master: *First thing, gentlemen salute the ladies.*

(The boys bow.)

Master: *Ladies salute the gentlemen*

(The girls curtsy.)

Master:

> *We are leaving now. So stand by the side of your partner and off down the road we go.*
>
> *We walk,*
>
> *We walk,*
>
> *We walk faster.*
>
> *We slow down.*

(Follow master's instructions.)

> *There are puddles on the road. We have to jump!*

(Everybody jumps.)

> *We walk,*
>
> *We walk,*
>
> *We walk faster.*
>
> *We slow down.*

> *There is a big tree fallen on the road. We have to walk backwards.*

(Everybody walks backwards.)

> *Now we can walk forward again.*
>
> *We walk,*
>
> *We walk,*
>
> *We walk faster.*
>
> *We slow down.*

Be careful! A snake is crossing the road.
(Everybody jumps really high and screams.)

The snake is gone.
We walk,
We walk,
We change direction.
We walk,
We change direction again.

Here comes the rain!
(Everybody puts their hands on their heads, while still "walking.")

It stopped! It was just a drizzle.
(Everybody cheers.)
We walk,
We walk,
We walk faster.
We slow down.

Now we are almost getting there.
But we still have to go through a tunnel.
(Boys on one side facing girls on the other side. Boys hold the girls' hands really high, making an arch. The last couple at the end of the line goes through the tunnel, and so on until the first couple goes through and becomes the first couple again.)

Hey, look at the railroad!
(Boys alternate with girls and form a long line, arms over the next one's shoulder.)

Here comes the train.
Chug, chug, chug.

We walk a little more,
We are there.

Now we can dance and party the whole night long!

FESTIVAL RECIPES

Food is very important at the festival. There are lots of typical foods offered during this time, many made of corn, manioc (cassava root), and coconut. Even in the big cities, these traditions are still preserved. Corn on the cob, cornmeal cake, peanut candy, and cocada are some of the most traditional items. Brigadeiro is a more recent invention, but it has become so popular that no party is considered complete without it. It is served at absolutely every birthday party, too.

Cocada

Ingredients:

> 6 cups sugar
>
> 2 cups water
>
> 4 cups shredded coconut

Instructions:

1. Grease a cookie sheet and set it aside.

2. In a large saucepan, combine the sugar and water and heat on medium, stirring until the mixture comes to a boil and the sugar has dissolved. Stop stirring and let simmer for 20 minutes.

3. Add the coconut and heat for 10 minutes, occasionally stirring, until you can see the bottom of the pan when you stir.

4. Remove the pan from the heat and pour the mixture onto the cookie sheet. Let cool, then cut into squares and remove the candy from the pan.

Brigadeiro

You can put each little ball into a tiny paper cup to serve.

Ingredients:

1 can condensed milk

1 tablespoon butter

2 tablespoons cocoa

granulated chocolate or confectioner's (powdered) sugar, for coating

Instructions:

1. Put all the ingredients in a saucepan except the granulated chocolate. Put the pan on medium heat and stir until you can see the bottom of the pan.

2. Pour the mixture into a dish. Roll it into small balls, slightly larger than marbles. Roll the balls in the granulated chocolate or powdered sugar.

Pumpkin Sweets

This recipe should make approximately 40 pumpkin balls.

Ingredients:

3 cups canned (or boiled and mashed) pumpkin

3 cups shredded coconut

1 cup honey (optional)

finely shredded coconut, for decoration

Instructions:

1. Put the pumpkin, coconut, and honey in a saucepan with a little water. Heat on medium, stirring constantly.

2. Cook until you can see the bottom of the pan when you stir. Let the mixture cool.

3. When the mixture is cool, roll it into little balls. You can use the shredded coconut for decoration.

Pamonhas

Pamonhas can be eaten cold or warm.

Ingredients:

> 12 cobs of corn (with the husks)
>
> 1 cup sugar
>
> 1 cup milk or coconut milk

Instructions:

1. Shuck the corn, setting aside the freshest looking husks. Scrape the corn from the cob and put it in a blender, along with the sugar and milk. Mix well.

2. Distribute the mixture among the husks and wrap into small bundles, tying them up with thin string.

3. Boil for one hour, then drain.

Cajuzinhos (Little Cashews)

Ingredients:

> 1 pound peanuts, toasted and ground
>
> 4 cups sugar
>
> powdered cocoa, enough to make mixture dark brown
>
> confectioner's (powdered) sugar, for decoration
>
> peanuts cut in half, for decoration

Instructions:

1. Mix together the peanuts, sugar, and cocoa until well blended. If the mixture becomes too hard or dry, you can blend in some water or milk.

2. Form the mixture into the shape of tiny cashews, roll them in the confectioner's sugar, and then stick one peanut half on the top side of each candy.

Dreams (Dumplings)

Livia says that her grandmother used to mix tiny pieces of apple into the dumplings before frying them!

Ingredients:

4 cups flour

4 tablespoons sugar

2 eggs

1 tablespoon vinegar

1 tablespoon baking soda

milk

sugar and cinnamon (2 to 1) for coating the dumplings (optional)

Instructions:

1. Combine the flour, sugar, eggs, and vinegar; mix well. Add the milk slowly, until you have a smooth mixture. Add the baking soda last.

2. Deep fry the mixture one spoonful at a time. Then roll the dumplings in the sugar and cinnamon mix.

3. Alternatively, you can make the dumplings larger, then cut them open and fill them with jam.

APPENDIX: NOTES ABOUT THE TALES

The intent of these tale notes is to give an idea of the distribution of these Brazilian tales throughout the world. Some traveled to Brazil from Europe, some from Africa. Some, such as the tales of the Curupira, are distinct to South America, yet sometimes utilize universal themes. Except where noted, these notes are by the editor.

The <u>motif numbers</u> given below are based on the Stith Thompson *Motif-Index of Folk-Literature* (Bloomington: Indiana University Press, 1966). Numbers that have an asterisk and are preceded by the word "MacDonald" are from *The Storyteller's Sourcebook: A Subject, Title, and Motif-Index to Folklore Collections for Children* by Margaret Read MacDonald (Detroit: Gale Research, 1982). These numbers have been extended from the Stith Thompson motif-index. In other words, the exact tale did not exist in Stith Thompson's index, so, using the decimal format set up by Thompson, MacDonald expanded the index. "MacDonald & Sturm" refers to a supplement published in 2000, *The Storyteller's Sourcebook: A Subject, Title and Motif-Index to Folklore Collections for Children: 1983–1999* by Margaret Read MacDonald and Brian Sturm (Detroit: Gale Research, 2001).

The <u>type numbers</u> mentioned refer to *The Types of the Folktale* by Antti Aarne and Stith Thompson (Helsinki: Suomalainen Tiedeakatemia, 1973). Also included are type numbers from Terrence Leslie Hansen, *The Types of the Folktale in Cuba, Puerto Rico, the Dominican Republic, and Spanish South America.* (Berkeley: University of California, 1957) and from Helen L. Flowers, *A Classification of the Folktale of the West Indies by Types and Motifs* (New York: Arno, 1980). Flowers's book contains both type and motif numbers.

Part 1: Magical Tales of the Rain Forest Peoples

The Creation of the Amazon River. This is an adaptation of a tale collected by Gustavo Barroso and included in his *Mythes, Contes et Légendes des Indiens*. A930 Origin of streams. A736.1.3 Sun and moon as lovers.

Star Fate of the Bororo Boys. *A761 Ascent to the stars. People or animals ascend to the sky and become stars.* Thompson cites versions from Estonia, India, Japan, Hawaii, Maori, Tonga, Australia, Eskimo, Africa (Ekoi), and South American Indian (Toba, Yuacari, Eastern Brazil, Tapirape, Aymara). Although this tale makes no mention of the Pleiades, many such tales state that the boys have become the Pleiades. *A773 Origin of the Pleiades.* Thompson cites versions from Lithuania, Siberia, India, China, Eskimo, Africa, North American Indian (Blackfoot), and South American Indian (Tarahumare, Tepehuane, Chaco, Pampean, Amazon). *R321 Escape to the stars.* Fugitives rise in the air and become stars. Thompson cites variants from Greece, India, Japan, Korea, Eskimo, North American Indian, and South American Indian (Chiriguano, Jivaro).

How the Night Came to Be (A Tupy myth). This myth is told by the Tupy people. It contains these motifs: *A1174 Origin of night. A1174.1 Night (darkness) in package. Released. A1174.1.2* Water Serpent's daughter weds man.* MacDonald cites a Brazilian variant of this tale from Mercedes Dorson and Jeanne Wilmot, *Tales from the Rain Forest: Myths and Legends from the Amazonian Indians of Brazil* (Ecco, 1997), 11–22. Margaret H. Lippert's *The Sea Serpent's Daughter* (Troll, 1993) is a picture book version of this tale. Another motif is *A1861 Creation of monkeys.*

The Wandering Head: How the Moon Came to Be (A Kaxinawa myth). The Kaxinawa, who live in the Acre forests along the Iboacu River, tell this strange tale. We have deleted from our version the incident in which the moon states that women will bleed with each new moon. *R261.1 Pursuit by rolling head.* The image of a pursuing rolling head (skull) seems popular in many cultures. Thompson cites sources from England, Japan, Native American, South American Indian (Chiriguano, Cashinawa, Chaco, Warrau, Shipaya, Tenetehara), and Africa (Congo). *E261.1 Wandering skull pursues man.* Thompson cites Indonesian and Zuñi versions. *G361.2 Great head as ogre. Head detached from body pursues or flies about doing damage.* Iroquois. Other motifs are *A731 Moon from object (person) thrown into sky. A755.7 Moon's waning caused by menstrual period. A747 Person transformed to moon.*

The Story of Mani (A Tupy myth). A story told by the Tupy people. *A2685.5 Origin of Manioc.* Thompson cites two versions, South American Indian (Paressi, Mataco). Also includes *T547 Birth from virgin.* Thompson cites South American Indian version (Chiriguano). MacDonald cites an Aymara version of this tale, which is quite similar to the Tupy version (Frances Carpenter, *South American Wonder Tales* [Follett, 1969], 57–63). Elsie Spicer Eels includes a somewhat different tale in *Tales from the Amazon* (Dodd, Mead, 1927), 179–193. Another quite different Brazilian tale of the origin of manioc from a maiden appears in *Jade and Iron: Latin American Tales from Two Cultures* by Patricia Aldana (Douglas and McIntyre, 1996), 6–8.

The Snake Eater (A Caxinauá tale). This tale was published by Clemens Bradenburger in *Lendas dos nossos índios* (Rio de Janeiro: F. Alves, 1931). This is motif *C221.1 Tabu: eating flesh of certain animal.* The husband here tricks the wife into eating the tabu snake meat.

The Story of the Vitória Régia, the Amazon Water Lily. This tale contains motif *C162.3 Tabu: marrying outside of group.* MacDonald & Sturm motif *A2666.8.1 Origin of water lily.* Mercedes Dorson and Jeanne Wilmot include a retelling of this tale in *Tales from the Rain Forest: Myths and Legends from the Amazonian Indians of Brazil* (Hopewell, N.J.: Ecco, 1997), 67–73.

The Hawk Husband (a myth from the Sauteré Maué). This tale was adapted from versions found in José Vieira Couto de Magalhães, *O selvagem* (São Paulo: Melhoramentos, 1935) and Hernâni Donato, *Contos dos meninos índios* (São Paulo: Melhoramentos, 1994). Couto de Magalhães collected this tale among natives of the Tocantins River valley, where he lived in 1865 for four months after a shipwreck by the Itaboca falls. Among the natives, abundance of food is the equivalent of riches, and it seems that, as in other civilizations, the ideal husband is a beautiful, rich, and valiant man. This includes *H422 Tests for true husbands.* It is interesting that though this was collected from indigenous peoples in 1865, the tale bears close resemblances to the Spanish/Arabic tale of the cockroach/ant who seeks a husband (*Z32.3 Little ant finds a penny, buys new clothes with it, and sits in her doorway. Various animals pass by and propose marriage*). How lucky we are that Couto de Magalhães was shipwrecked and stuck in the Tocantin valley for four months with nothing to do but collect folktales!

The Story of Guaraná. *B613.1 Snake paramour. T515 Impregnation through glance.* Interestingly, this unusual motif has been collected in England, Rumania, and the Cape Verde Islands. Stith Thompson also cites a version of this motif from the Native American Yana tribe. *C225 Tabu: eating certain fruit.* Eating of certain nuts is tabu in this tale. The mother in this tale plants her dead son's body and from it springs the first guarana plant. *A2611.0.1 Plants from grave of dead person or animal.* Stith Thompson cites variants of this motif from the South American Toba, Paressi, and Cashinawa peoples. The guarana is a shrub or small tree whose berry is a source of caffeine.

> *Source:* Nunes Pereira, *Moronguetá: Um decameron indígena* (Rio de Janeiro: Civilização Brasileira, 1967).

Part 2: Animal Tales from the Rain Forest

Turtle and Onça, the Jaguar. This tale was collected by the following scholars who studied the native oral tradition of Brazil: Gustavo Barroso, *Mythes, contes et légendes des indiens; folk-lore brésilien* (Paris: A. Ferroud, 1930); Charles Frederik Hart, *Os mitos amazônicos da tartaruga* (Recife: Arquivo Público Estadual, 1952); and José Vieira Couto de Magalhães, *O selvagem* (Melhoramentos, 1935). The major motif in this story seems to have many African antecedents. The motif is *K1775 Bluff: insult repeated as harmless remark. The trickster makes an insulting remark, but when called on to repeat what he said he changes it so as to turn aside wrath.* Thompson cites tales from Indonesia, the Basuto, Benga, Yoruba, Ibo, Kaffir, Ila, the West Indies, and the "Nun's Priest's Tale" in Chaucer. Flowers cites one tale from Montserat ("Terycoma and Lion"). MacDonald's *Storyteller's Sourcebook* cites a Russian version (fox), and a Liberian tale described here *K1775.1* MacDonald. Turtle makes flute of jackal's thighbone, sings of this. Jackal brother asks what he sings, says "the bone of a cow makes me a flute."* This tale bears similarity also to *K1715.3 The wolf flees from the wolf-head.*

How Agouti Fooled Onça. *K713.1.1 Animal allows himself to be tied so as to avoid being carried off by storm.* Thompson cites variants from Africa (Wute), Georgia (Brer Rabbit), West Indies, Jamaica, and Cape Verde Islands. Flowers cites variants from Trinidad (Lion and Zaen), Grenada (Lion and Zaen), Jamaica (Anansi and Lion and Anansi and Tiger), St.Thomas (Lion and Annancy), and Antigua (Nancy and Lion). MacDonald cites variants from Puerto Rico, the West Indies, and Georgia (Brer Rabbit). William Faulkner's *Brer Tiger and the Big Wind* (Morrow, 1995) is a picture book using this motif. The tale also appears in Kantchil Mousedeer lore of Malaysia and Indonesia. *K581.2 Briar-patch punishment for rabbit. By expressing horror of being thrown into the briar patch, he induces his captor into doing so. He runs off.* MacDonald cites variants from Shona, Cherokee, African-American (Brer Rabbit and others), and West Virginia. In addition, Thompson cites sources from Missouri French, Louisiana Creole, Indonesia, Rhodesia, Zanzibar, Jamaica, and the West Indies. This motif often appears with the tar-baby motif, but can appear alone or in conjunction with other motifs. *K455.2 Supper won by disguising as an invited guest.* Thompson cites one variant, from Jamaica. Hansen: *Type 74A Rabbit persuades tiger that storm is approaching* cites tales from Argentina (2), Peru, Puerto Rico (11), and Venezuela. Flowers cites two variants from Jamaica (turtle, fish), Antigua (hare), and Barbados (hare).

Jaguar and Goat. *K1715.3.2* Goat begins to build a house. Tiger finds foundation and adds to it. Each thinks god is helping with the work. Discovering their "partner" they agree to live together. Goat brings in dead tiger and tiger flees.* This tale seems to be clearly of African origin. MacDonald cites sources from Haiti, Brazil (deer and jaguar), Africa, Galla (monkey and hyena), Congo (squirrel and leopard), and Congo (bushbuck and leopard). MacDonald & Sturm cite Tanzania, Swahili (hare and leopard), and Africa (wildcat and hyena).

How Turtle Tricked Onça. This tale was collected by Charles Frederik Hart, *Os Mitos Amazônicas da Tartaruga* (Arquivo Público Estadual, 1952). *K343.3 Companion sent away so that rascal may steal common food supply.* Stith Thompson cites sources with this motif from: India, Cameroon, Georgia(U.S.), Virginia, South Carolina, and Cape Verde Islands. Flowers cites sources from Jamaica (horse and Anansi) and Martinique (elephant and rabbit).

Crab with the Flying Eyes (a Taulipang myth). This story was collected among the Taulipang, a native tribe who live near the Guiana, by Theodor Kock-Grünberg. It is recorded in his *Von Rorima zum Orinoco* (Stuttgart: Strecker und Schorder, 1924). This story takes as its starting point the ability that crabs have to project their eyes. The tale also appears in Alberto da Costa Silva, *Antologia de lendas do índio brasileiro* (Rio de Janeiro: INL, 1957). *J2423 The Eye-juggler. A trickster sees a man throwing his eyes into the air and replacing them. He also receives this power but he must not use the power beyond a specified number of times. When he does so, he loses his eyes. He usually gets animal eyes as substitutes (E781.1)* This is a widespread Native American tale. MacDonald & Sturm cite four Coyote variants, and one about Iktomi. "Crab with the Flying Eyes" applies this motif to a crab's extended eye formation. *J2423.2* Jaguar threatens and crab makes Jaguar's eyes go sailing.* MacDonald & Sturm cite one variant, the retelling in MacDonald's *Twenty Tellable Tales.* MacDonald created her version from Valery Carrick's *Picture Folk-Tales* and from the Kock-Grünberg version mentioned above. Quite likely Carrick's version also came from Kock-Grünberg.

Curupira and the Hunter. This story was published in many versions by Gustavo Barroso in his *Mythes, contes et legends des indiens* (Ferroud, 1930). For a quite different Curupira tale see "The Curupira" in *Earth Care: World Folktales to Talk About* by Margaret Read MacDonald (Linnet Books, 1992). *G524 Ogre deceived into stabbing himself. He imitates the hero, who has stabbed a bag of blood.* This is a common theme in European folklore. It appears in "Jack the Giant Killer," among others. MacDonald cites also a Brazilian variant (Frances Carpenter, *South American Wonder Tales* [Doubleday, 1969]). *C420.1 Man (woman) persuaded to reveal fatal secret.* This tale also bears similarities to *B216 Knowledge of animal language,* a widely told European folktale in which the wife insists until the husband tells her his secret.

Part 3: Animal Tales from Africa and Europe

A Party in Heaven. Ana tells us: "This is one of the most popular tales in Brazil. The origin of 'Party in Heaven' is an object of prolonged discussions. Similar stories are present in the body of Eastern and Western fables. Present in the Indian *Calila e Dima* (a widely disseminated body of stories in the thirteenth century in Europe and Asia), this story was selected by La Fontaine, who used the same motif in *La Tortue et les Deux*

Canards. The theme is basically the same: an animal that crawls cannot dream of flight and elevation. The moral is simple: the fall is the punishment of the ambitious.

"The South-American versions show the *Jabuti* or Frog hiding inside a basket or a guitar that belonged to Buzzard, an eagle or a *garça*. When they go back, they are punished for their spunk, thrown back to earth by the injured animal. The intention of the harm is not present in classical versions. The animal that hides itself to go to heaven, thus, is a South American element.

"The change of animals is quite frequent in stories. Aesop's eagle corresponds to the geese and ducks in versions from India. The Eagle is the avenger from Gascogne (Spain/France). In Brazil, Buzzard is the strong, powerful bird that is able to carry the reptile. The Turtle, from Eastern versions, becomes the restless Fox in Spain. In Africa, there is the story of Jackal and the Eagle. To avenge the death of its young ones, eaten by Jackal, Eagle carries the creature up in heaven and then drops it. Jackal falls, screaming: 'Let me fall on the water or over a haystack.' But it falls on a rock and dies.

"In Brazil, Turtle or Jabuti or Frog were used because they well symbolized the careful relation to the ground. Another reason has to do with an etiological intention. Both Frog and Turtle have a skin or shell that seems to be patched. Under Christian influence, there are many versions in Brazil showing Our Lady's interference. She prevents the Jabuti from dying and heals its hurts."

K1041 Borrowed Feathers. Dupe lets himself be carried aloft by bird and dropped. Type 225. This is a very common folktale motif, though the dupe often is just going for a ride, rather than attending a party in the heavens. MacDonald cites versions from Liberia, the Antilles, Haiti, Hausa, West Africa, East Africa, Eskimo, African-American, Chuckee, Ukrainian, Hottentot, Palestinian, Berber-Kabyl, and Aesop. Flying to get food appears in a Liberian (Mano) tale in which Oldman God tells birds to each give turtle a feather so he can fly up and eat cork seeds in heaven. In another Liberian tale, ricebird lends catfish feathers to fly to farmer's tapping bowl at top of palm wine tree. A Jamaican tale shows Anansi borrowing feathers to fly to dokanoo tree. And a tale from Haiti and Jamaica shows turtle borrowing pigeon feathers to fly to a cornfield. In a West Indian tale, Anansi flies to another island to feed. And in a Hausa tale, gizo spider is carried by crows to a fig tree. Closest to our tale is one from the Antilles in which Turtle borrows feathers to attend a feast in heaven. (Dorothy Sharp Carter, *Greedy Mariani and Other Folktales of the Antilles* [Atheneum, 1974], 46–61). MacDonald & Sturm add versions from Mexico, Africa (Khoikhoi), Native American (Iktomi, Cherokee, Zuñi, Cree), Liberia (Dan), and African-American. Some feast-associated tales are *K1041.3* MacDonald. Tio Conejo (hare) taken to feast in heaven by Tio Buzzard. Buzzard tries to drop Conejo but Conejo hits Buzzard over the head with guitar and holds Buzzard's wings outstretched so unconscious buzzard can glide to earth.* From Nicaragua: Diane Wolkstein, *Cool Ride in the Sky* (Random House, 1973). *K1041.1.7* MacDonald & Sturm. Spider borrows feathers to attend feast in heaven. Claims name is "All of you" (K359.2) and eats all food. Feathers taken back. Spider falls.* From Liberia, Dan: Won-Ldy Paye, *Why Leopard Has Spots* (Fulcrum, 1998), 23–30. *K1041.1.10* MacDonald & Sturm. Wolf borrows feathers from birds to* *fly over water to a feast. He ridicules each bird so they take back their feathers and wolf cannot fly back.* From African-American: Virginia Hamilton, *The People Could Fly* (Knopf, 1995), 43–48. Hansen: *Type 59. Fox accepts condor's invitation to celebration* cites Peru (1) and Puerto Rico (1).

The Cockroach's Wedding. Livia tells us: "This is another very popular tale in Brazil. It was brought by the Portuguese, who named it the 'História da Carochinha.' In Brazilian folklore, 'Historia da Carochinha' became an expression that encompasses most wonder tales. Carochas include elves, witches, demons, and also unappealing insects like the cockroach. Originally this was an Aryan story that spread in all the Western European countries with few variations. In some versions, the protagonist is an old maid who plans to get married; she dresses herself up and tries to get a bridegroom. Sometimes, it is a mouse. In Brazil, it became a cockroach.

"In the Panchatantra we found the following version, which we reproduce here in a concise way: 'A holy man kept a pretty little she-mouse in his house that had fallen from the claws of a hawk. Through his virtues and powers, he managed to transform her into a beautiful girl and raised her as a daughter. When she was grown up, the girl asked him to be married. Father searched the sun, but he is refused because he is too hot. Sun points that the cloud is stronger than him because it is able to screen his brightness. Cloud says that the wind is stronger. Wind says that the hill is stronger. The hill says that the mouse is stronger. The mouse is chosen and the girl begs her adoptive father to let her reassume her former shape in order to marry her beloved.' In both versions the mouse is the chosen one. In the Panchatantra happiness is assured because the girl breaks the spell before the wedding and becomes an equal to her bridegroom.

"In 'História da Carochinha' and other Greek-Roman versions, the final result is always painful disillusionment or widowhood. The mouse is beaten by his own nature, falls in the pan, and dies. This idea is present in classical texts (Aesop and Romulus). There is one fable that tells that Jove turned a Fox into a woman. The Fox had longed to marry him. But after the change is done, Fox can't resist the sight of a bug, jumps onto it, and is sent away by Jove. The conclusion: it is impossible to deny one's nature. A fox will always be a fox, even if it is in the shape of a woman.

"La Fontaine certainly got inspiration from this tale to write his fable of Cat turned into woman. The metamorphoses do not alter one's character.

"Closest to the version we know of Dona Baratinha is a story that is in the Mahabharata: 'The daughter of the king of the frogs takes human shape. She gets married and explains that she will never be able to get close to a pond or a lake. A courtesan, envious, takes her to the pond where she dives and become a frog forever.' João Ratão, the holy man's daughter, the princess of frogs, La Fontaine's cat, Aesop's fox change their shapes, become more attractive, but do not resist temptation."

Z32.3 Little ant finds a penny, buys new clothes with it, and sits in her doorway. Various animals pass by and propose marriage. She asks what they do at night. Each one replies with its characteristic sound and none pleases her but the quiet little mouse, whom she marries. She leaves him to tend the stew and he falls in and drowns.

She weeps and, on hearing the reason, bird cuts off its beak, dove cuts off its tail, etc. The tale often appears without the chain-from-weeping addition. This tale has Persian, Turkish, and Arabic variants, and is known throughout the Spanish-Portuguese speaking world. MacDonald cites sources from Portugal, Puerto Rico, Mexico, Spain, Persia, and Turkey. *Type 2023 Little Ant Finds a Penny, Buys New Clothes with it, and Sits in Her Doorway* cites French, Spanish, Catalan, Italian, Turkish, Cuban, and Puerto Rican variants. Hansen: *Type 2023* cites versions from Cuba (2) and Puerto Rico (10).

The Bald Chick. Stith Thompson's Motif-Index cites one version from India under Z52 Bird avenges caged mate. Arms self and proclaims war with king. Collects cat, ants, rope, club and river. The tale is popular in children's books, and MacDonald cites variants from France (Drakestail), Spain (Medio Pollito), Switzerland (Red Chick), Hungary (Little Rooster and the Turkish Sultan), Portugal (Tipsy Rooster), and Burma (a Thumbling), along with one Brazilian variant and variants from Poland and Russia.

Monkey and the Corn Cake. J1577 Deceptive invitation to feast. K714.2 Victim tricked into entering box. This is reminiscent of the tale of the wife who hides her suitors in various places in the house. The husband arrives and chases them off. K1218.1 (Type 1730.

Part 4: Tales of Enchantment

The Louse-skin Chair. *H522.1.1 Test: guessing nature of certain skin—louse-skin. Louse (flea)* [sic] *is fattened and its skin made into coat (drum, etc.). Type 621 The Louse Skin.* This is a well-known European tale, told also in India. Thompson cites variants from Brittany, Italy, India, and the Philippines. MacDonald cites versions from Puerto Rico, Spain (tambourine), Bulgaria, Greece, and one of unnamed European source about slippers made from a giant pet caterpillar's skin. MacDonald & Sturm add variants from France and Spain. Hansen: *Type 621* cites five Puerto Rican variants.

H1112 Task: herding rabbits. H1112.0.1* Old woman befriended by youngest brother gives him magic whistle to herd hares. He wins princess. MacDonald cites a Gypsy version from Syria and a Finnish version. Flowers cites versions of this tale from Dominica (2) and Andros Island. *H1045 Filling a sack full of lies (truths). H1045.0.1* Brother aids old woman and receives magic whistle which calls hares to it. Type 570 The rabbit-herd* cites sources of this tale from Germany (Grimms), Finland, Sweden, Estonia, Livonia, Lithuania, Lapland, Norway, Denmark, Iceland, Ireland, France, Spain, Netherlands, Austria, Italy, Hungary, Czech, Slovenia, Serbo-Croatia, Poland, Russia, Greece, Turkey, Cape Verde Islands, the West Indies, Spanish-American, and Portuguese-American. MacDonald cites versions from Norway, France, Appalachia, Scandinavia, and Spain. MacDonald & Sturm add an African-American variant.

The Three Sisters and the Children with Golden Stars on Their Brows. *N455.4 King overhears girl's boast as to what she would do as queen.* MacDonald cites variants from Greece, Arabia, Turkey, India, Rumania, Bulgaria, Gypsy, and Liberia (Loma). MacDonald & Sturm cite variants from Germany, Egypt, and Russia. *Type 707 Three Golden Sons. The queen bears marvelous children. They are stolen away. The queen is banished. The quest for the speaking bird, the singing tree, and the water of life* cites variants from Germany(Grimm); Spain, Finland, Estonia, Livonia, Lithuania, Sweden, Norway, Denmark, Iceland, Ireland, Basque, France, Austria, Italy, Rumania, Hungary, Czech, Slovenia, Serbo-Croatia, Russia, Greece, Turkey, Chile, the Dominican Republic, Cape Verde Islands, the West Indies, Native American, and African. *H1321.1 Quest for Water of Life. D231.2 Transformation: man to marble column.* The tale's quest motif is similar to that in the Arabian Nights tale of the quest for the singing bird, the talking tree, and the golden fountain. Hansen: *Type 707* cites many variants of this tale from Chile (14), the Dominican Republic (12), and Puerto Rico (9).

Princess Toad. *MacDonald B641.0.1* The Mouse (Cat, Frog, etc.) as bride. The youngest of three brothers succeeds best in the quest set by his father. He brings the best cloth, the most beautiful bride, etc. The mouse (cat, etc.) who has helped him changes herself into a beautiful maiden.* This tale is famous throughout Europe, with variants in Asia and Latin America. MacDonald cites variants of this with a frog bride from Italy, Switzerland, Philippines (Visaya), England, Germany (Grimm), Russia, Ukraine, and Yugoslavia. Also listed are variants from Portugal (cow, cat), France (mouse), Finland (mouse), Sweden (mouse), India (monkey), Italy (monkey), Uigur (monkey), Germany (Grimm, cat), France (cat), Denmark (cat), Sweden (fox), and Egypt (tortoise). MacDonald & Sturm add variants from Chile (frog), Greece (frog), Finland (mouse), Norway (tiny maid), and Portugal (spider). *Type 402 The Mouse (Cat, Frog, etc.) as Bride* cites variants from Germany, Finland, Estonia, Livonia, Lithuania, Lapland, Sweden, Denmark, Ireland, France, Flemish, Austria, Italy, Hungary, Czech, Slovenia, Serbo-Croatia, Poland, Russia, Greece, Turkey, India, Chile, the Dominican Republic, Brazil, and the West Indies. Hanson: *Type 402* cites two tales from the Dominican Republic.

The Singing Grasses. The motif of a murdered person turning to grass (tree, bird, etc.) and singing of murder is common in European and Latin American folklore. *N271 Murder will out. E631 Reincarnation in plant (tree) growing from grave. E632 Reincarnation as musical instrument. The Singing Bone. A musical instrument made from the bones of a murdered person, or from a tree growing from the grave, speaks and tells of the crime.* Thompson cites variants from England, Brittany, Africa (Ibo, Fang), India, and Japan. *Type 780B The Speaking Hair. A stepmother buries a girl alive. Her hair grows as wheat or bush and sings her misfortunes. Thus she is discovered and dug up alive. The stepmother is buried in the same hole.* Aarne-Thompson cite versions from Spain, France, Catalan, Puerto Rico, and North Africa for this tale type, which is almost identical to our Brazilian variant. Hansen: *Type 780B* cites variants from Cuba (2) and Puerto Rico (11). The tale bears resemblance to *D1316.5.0.3 Magic speaking reed* *(tree) betrays secret. King has whispered secret to hoe in the ground. Reed growing from this hole tells his secret.*

Livia's sources tell us: "This story, of Portuguese origin, arrived in Brazil with different versions. In some of them, the girl's hair spread all around the fig tree and from inside the earth came a voice that begged: 'Dear Father, don't cut my hair.' In some versions, the girl is not saved from death. The story belongs to the same cycle as 'The Spanish Flower of Lililá,' of the Costa Rican 'Niños sin mama' tales. In common they have the motif of plants that tell to the world a secret, as in the tale of King Midas and the barber *(D1316.5.0.)*."

The Golden Jars. This is a variant of a much-told tale, with many European variants. The tale also appears throughout the world. This Brazilian tale seems unique in that the magical old woman starts the train of events by stealing a golden jar from the home of the girls. The device of the string bean is also unusual. Livia was unable to determine if the girls were to snap the string bean from the vine as they carried it home or to string the bean. As the bean was said to be dried, we are assuming it was to be snapped off the vine. *Type 489 The Spinning-Women by the Spring. The Kind and Unkind Girls. Type 402 The Black and the White Bride.* For an entire treatise on this tale, see Warren Roberts, *The Tale of the Kind and the Unkind Girl; Aa-Th 480 and Related Tales* (Berlin: De Gruyter, 1958). *The Types of the Folktale* cites variants from Norway, Germany, Finland, Estonia, Livonia, Lithuania, Lapp, Icelandic, Danish, Irish, English French Spanish, Catalan, Flemish, Austrian, Italian, Sicilian, Rumanian, Hungarian, Czech, Slovenia, Serbo-Croatia, Polish, Russian, Greek Turkish, India; Indonesian; the Dominican Republic, Puerto Rico, and the West Indies. Under motif *Q2.1 Kind and unkind girls.* MacDonald describes fifty-four versions of this tale; most are European, but variants from Japan, Haiti, Xhosa, Venezuela, Burma, and Sierra Leone are also found. In addition to many European variants, MacDonald & Sturm cite versions from Chile, African-American, African, Tamilnadu, Karnataka (India), and Siberia.

The Old Lady in the Woods. *Type 442 The Old Man in the Forest. The maiden disenchants a prince whom an evil woman has transformed into a tree. She gets the magic ring from the old woman's house. The Types of the Folktale cites sources from Scotland, Ireland, Poland, Russia, and Germany (Grimm). D1776 Magic key D1176; D1076 Magic ring; D1383.1 Tree opens and conceals fugitive; D1556 Self-opening tree trunk.; D950 Magic Tree; D1556.2 Tree opens its trunk to give shelter to abandoned girls. (from India); D799.3 Attendants of disenchanted person automatically disenchanted. (German, Grimm); D771.10 Disenchantment by ring. (German, Grimm.; D154.1 Transformation: Man to dove. (German, South American Indian Chiriguano; India; Spanish; Greek; and D215 Transformation: Man to tree.*

The Princess with the Seven Pairs of Shoes. *Type 306 The danced-out Shoes. MacDonald F1015.1.1 The danced-out shoes. Every morning girl's shoes are danced to pieces.* MacDonald cites Grimm (Twelve Dancing Princesses), Denmark, Bulgaria, Portugal,

---

Turkey, and France. *D2131 Magic underground journey. D1980 Escape of girl foiled by hero's refusal to take narcotic.* This Brazilian tale is unusual in that there is only one princess, rather than seven. The addition of Calicote, the imp in the chest, is also unique. And the golden turkey feet and silver chicken feet are a delightful addition!

The Fish Mother. This motif often appears in conjunction with the Cinderella story. The fish helper is unusual but occurs in similar tales from Vietnam. (See MacDonald & Sturm R221Qb*) and China (MacDonald R221J*), but in these variants the fish is a pet, rather than the reincarnated mother. *B313 Helpful animal reincarnation of parent. The dead mother appears to the heroine in the form of an animal. E323.2 Dead mother returns to help persecuted daughter. E631 Reincarnation in plant growing from grave.*

Part 5: Pedro Malasartes, the Trickster

For more Latin American tales about Pedro Malasartes, see Ramón A. Laval, *Cuentos de Pedro de Urdemalas* (Santiago de Chile: Cruz de Sur, 1943) and Julio Aramburu, *Las hazañas de Pedro Urdemalas: cuentos para niños* (Buenos Aires: El Ateneo, 1944).

Pedro Malasartes in the Bag. *K842 Dupe persuaded to take prisioner's place in a sack: killed. The trickster is to be thrown into the sea. The trickster keeps shouting that he does not want to go to heaven (or marry the princess); the dupe gladly substitutes for him.* Sometimes in conjunction with *K1051 Diving for sheep. A dupe persuaded that sheep have been lost in river. Type 1535 The Rich and the Poor Peasant.* This longer tale sometimes includes the "bag" and "sheep in river" motifs. MacDonald cites many European variants of this: Georgia (Russia), Scandinavia, Bulgaria, Celtic, Irish, French, German (Grimms), Belgium, Appalachia (U.S.), and India. Similar tales from Ethiopia, Masai, Native American, and China. MacDonald & Sturm add tales from Chile, Italy, and Russia.

Pedro Malasartes and the Doll Murderer. *K2150 Innocent made to appear guilty.* The "doll murderer" bears a close resemblance to motif *K2151*, except that the corpse is a fake in our story. *K2151 The corpse handed around. The thrice-killed corpse. Dupes are accused of murder when the corpse is left with them. The trickster is paid to keep silent. Type 1537 The Corpse Killed Five Times. The corpse on the horse in the sleigh, in the boat.* The most well known version in the United States is the Appalachian tale of "Old Dry Frye" (Richard Chase, *Grandfather Tales* [Houghton Mifflin, 1948]). The notion of a corpse (or fake corpse) re-killed via a trickster's ruse seems a popular motif throughout the world. Thompson cites variants from Turkey, France, Spain, Italy, India, Japan, Norway, England, Korea, Micmac, Zuñi, and Ojibwa. Hanson: *Type 1531 Corpse Killed Five Times* cites variants from Puerto Rico, the Dominican Republic, and Cuba (5).

Pedro Malasartes Herds Pigs. *K404.1 Tails in ground. Thief steals animals and sticks severed tails into the ground, claiming that animals have escaped underground. Type 1004 Hogs in the Mud; Sheep in the Air. K404.1* is a widespread motif. Thompson cites variants from Iceland, Missouri French, Louisiana Creole, Indonesia, Africa (Vai), Georgia (Brer Rabbit), Virginia, South Carolina, the Bahamas, Jamaica, and the Cape Verde Islands. MacDonald adds a Danish version. Sometimes combined with *K1354.1 Both? The youth is sent to the house to get two articles.* A tale with both motifs that is very similar to our Brazilian story appears in Yolanda Pino-Saavedra, *Folktales of Chile* (University of Chicago, 1967), 214–215. Hansen: *Type 1004* cites Puerto Rico (3), Chile, and Argentina.

Pedro Malasartes Sells Rabbits. *K131.1.1 Alleged speaking hare sold as messenger. Usually one hare released and accomplice produces second saying it delivered message.* A popular trickster motif. MacDonald cites sources from Afghanistan, Georgia (Russia), China, Bulgaria, and Russia. *Type 1539 Cleverness and Gullibility* lists versions from Turkey, Finland, Estonia, Livonia, Lithuania, Lapland, Finland, Norway, Denmark, Scotland, Ireland, England, Catalan, the Netherlands, Flemish, German, Italian, Sicilian, Rumanian, Hungarian, Czech, Slovenian, Serbo-Croatian, Russian, Greek, India, Indonesian, Chinese, Argentina, Chile, Cuba, Puerto Rico, West Indies, Native American, and African. Hansen: *Type 1563* cites Chile and Puerto Rico (3). Flowers cites tales with this type from Puerto Rico (4) and Guadalupe. Our Brazilian tale adds a second motif, *G524 Ogre deceived into stabbing himself. He imitates the hero, who has stabbed a bag of blood.* This motif appeared also in the Curupira tale in this collection.

Part 6: Scary Tales

The Skull Takes Revenge. *C13 Offended skull. A skull (statue) is invited to dinner. Attends the dinner and takes his host off to the other world.* Thompson cites variants from Germany, Spain, Italy, and France. *E238 Dinner with the dead. Dead man is invited to dinner. Takes his host off to other world.* Thompson cites variants from Brittany, Lithuania, Estonia, Spain, Greenland Eskimo, and the United States. *Type 470 Friends in Life and Death* includes this motif joined with several others. *E235.5 Return from dead to punish kicking of skull.* Thompson cites one Tlingit variant. Hansen: *Type 835 Skull or ghost is invited to dine* cites tales from Chile and the Dominican Republic. However, in these tales the man seems to escape with his life by wearing a talisman.

The Devil in a Bottle. *K717 Deception into a bottle (vessel).* Sometimes the demon/giant has come out of the bottle and is tricked back in. In other cases the demon/giant is tricked into showing how small it can make itself. *K722 Giant tricked into becoming mouse* also uses this trick. *Type 331 The Spirit in the Bottle* cites sources from Germany (Grimm), Finland, Sweden, Estonia, Lithuania, Sweden, Denmark, Ireland,

France, Spain, Catalan, Italy, Hungary, Czech, Slovenia, Serbo-Croatia, American Indian (Pochulta), Argentina, and Puerto Rico. It is a favorite motif in the adventures of the Chinese Monkey King, Sun Wu Kung, and MacDonald cites variants from Japan, the Bahamas, Africa, Russia, Switzerland, China, and England. Another motif in this tale is *H1023.2 Task: carrying water in a sieve.* Hansen: *Type 331* cites one Puerto Rican source.

The Headless Mule. *G211.1.2 Witch as mule.* There are many tales in which a man is transformed into a horse, donkey, or mule. *D132.2 Man transformed to mule.* However, this story is unusual in that the woman seems to turn into a mule each night. It feels more like a tale about a ghost donkey. *E402.2.2 Ghost donkey,* except that in this case the horrifying mule can be turned back into a beautiful lady. The headless horse/donkey/mule motif appears in various tales. *E423.1.1.3.3 Revenant as headless horse* and *E501.4.2.7 Headless horse in wild hunt* are found in England. From Japan and Scandinavia come tales of the *E521.1 Headless ghost of horse.* But our Brazilian tale is closest to *G211.1.1.1 Witch in form of headless horse.*

Creature of the Night. A tale collected in Maranhão in the North of Brazil. The chant uses a mixture of Portuguese and native words. The repeated singing in this tale is similar to the eaten-monkey tale in "The Old Lady and the Monkey," *Z13.5.* It reminds one also of the Australian tale, "The Hobyahs," in which a dog is de-limbed until he can no longer bark and scare off the monsters. (Joseph Jacobs, *English Folk and Fairy Tales* [Putnam, n.d.]). MacDonald *B332.1* Too watchful dog killed.

The Old Lady and the Monkey. This is the famous tar-baby story, which has many variants in African and African-American lore. *K741 Capture by tar baby.* MacDonald cites versions from Yoruba (frog), Georgia (Brer Rabbit), the American South (Possum catches rabbit), Cherokee (Rabbit), Swahili (rabbit), Rhodesia (rabbit caught by tortoise), Congo (jackal), West Africa (hare caught by elephant), Ashanti (Anansi the spider), Africa (squirrel), West Africa (gum doll), Nigeria (tortoise), Philippines, Visaya (ape), Native American (skunk), and Indonesia (Giant). *MacDonald K741.0.12* Monkey picking bananas for old woman gives her only poor half. She catches with wax boy. Monkeys make tower to sky and plead to sun to melt wax figure. It does and monkeys gain control of bananas.* A Brazilian variant appears in two children's books: in Shirlee Newman, *Folk Tales of Latin America* (Bobbs-Merrill, 1962), 61–66; and Rose Dobbs, *Once Upon a Time* (Random House, 1950). 60–66. In the story in our collection this story is combined with MacDonald *Motif Z13.5* Fish calls "take me home," "cook me," "eat me." Eaten. "I got you now, Peter." Peter is never seen again.* MacDonald cites one U.S. version; MacDonald & Sturm cite a variant from Uttar Pradesh, India and two African-American variants. The motif of a tricky animal swallowed who calls from the stomach and escapes is found in several African cultures, and in Arabic, Indian-Pakistani, and Spanish cultures, as well as in England. Examples are the Spanish variant MacDonald *Z49.3.1* The Picaro Bird. . . . . is* *caught, cooked, eaten, causes king to vomit. . . .* and the Pakistani variant *Z49.3.2 Toontoony Pie. Bird . . . swallowed, flies out of king's nose.* Hansen cites many variants under *Type 175* but most are rabbit and tar-baby tales and none mention an old woman and monkey. Flowers lists thirty-five versions of this tale type. Most feature rabbit, a few feature Anansi, and some feature humans. One tale from Guadalupe features a thieving monkey and the king's daughter, but with a "guess-the-girl's-name" ending.

The Creature of Fire. This unusual tale features a giant with fiery eyes. *F531.1.1.2 Giant with large gleaming eyes. F531.1.3 Eyes of live coals. F541.1.1 Eyes flash fire. The man learns a lesson about his miserliness. W 151 Greed.* As with many of the Amazonian tribal tales, this seems unique from the rest of world folk literature.

The Beetle Man. *B653 Marriage to insect in human form.* Many tales are told of witches and devils who leave their beds at night to prowl, but the use of a beetle in this tale seems unique. The beetle's cry for blood reminds one of the vampire motif. *E251 Vampire. Corpse which comes from grave at night and sucks blood.*

The Girl and the Kibungo. *G312 Cannibal ogre.* This tale includes the repeated refrains so common in African story-songs. The untranslatable "Kibungo terere" is likely an African dialect. The Kibungo appears also in a Brazilian folktale in Helen East, *The Singing Sack* (London: A & C. Black, 1989), 32–35, but in that tale he is tricked into dancing, while Jabuti and other animals escape.

The Kibungo and the Boy with the Sack Full of Feathers. *G312 Cannibal ogre. D1375.6 Magic object causes feathers to grow on person.* This most unusual story shows the boy collecting two feathers from each bird without harming them, then giving them to his people when in danger. The feathers allow them to grow wings and fly to escape. An African-American motif in which slaves escape through sudden magic flight occurs in the title story of Virginia Hamilton's *The People Could Fly* (New York: Knopf, 1985), although in this story no feathers or helpful young boy are involved. Also includes the widespread ogre-catching trick: *K735 capture in pitfall.* The repeated singing refrains lend the story similarity to African story-songs.

Part 7: Death Tales from Brazil

How the Blacksmith Fooled Death. *Q565 Man admitted neither to heaven nor hell. Type 330. MacDonald Q565A The Smith and the Devil. Type 330A The Smith and the Devil (Death).* MacDonald includes variants from Appalachian, Afro-American, French, Welsh, Norwegian, Slovenian, Irish, Czech, and Italian sources. MacDonald & Sturm include variants from Chile and Germany. *The Types of the Folktale* includes variants from thirteen European countries, along with variants from the United States, Argentina, Chile, Colombia, the Dominican Republic, and Puerto Rico. Several variants from Spain are cited. The tale clearly has European (probably Portuguese) roots. In most variants the smith tricks Death (or the Devil) with three tricky objects, usually a chair, bush, and sack. This Brazilian tale instead uses *D1415.2 Magical instrument causes person to dance*. This is also a popular motif in European folktales.

The Good Minister and Death. *MacDonald/Sturm Z111.9 * Death seen at bazaars and feared. Flees to Samarra. Death had appointment with him there*. This is very old motif, popular in the Middle East. The man meets Death in Baghdad or another city and Death is startled. The man flees to the city of Samarra and Death is glad to see him arrive, as he had an appointment with him in Samarra. See Robert San Souci, *More Short and Shivery* (New York: Delacorte, 1994), 4 for a Persian version of this tale. The story is usually known as "Appointment in Samarra" and was used as the evocative title of John O'Hara's novel *Appointment in Samarra*.

Aunt Misery's Pear Tree. *MacDonald, Z111.2.1.1* Death personified. Aunt Misery granted a wish by sheltered pilgrim. Pear tree from which one may not descend until she wishes. Death is caught.* MacDonald cites variants from Portugal, Puerto Rico, and Haiti.

BIBLIOGRAPHY

Amaral, Amadeu. *Tradições populares*. São Paulo: Ed. HUCITEC, 1982.

Aramburu, Julio. *Laz hazañas de Pedro Urdemalas: Cuentos para niños*. Buenos Aires: El Ateneo, 1944.

Araújo, Alceu Maynard. *Folclore nacional*. São Paulo: Melhoramentos, 1964.

Barroso, Gustavo. *Mythes, contes et légendes des indiens: Folk-lore Bréslien*. Paris: A. Ferroud, 1930.

Bradenburger, Clemens. *Lendas dos nossos índios*. Rio de Janeiro: F. Alves, 1931.

Braga, Teófilo. *Contos tradicionais do povo português*. Lisboa: Publicações D. Quixote, 1987.

Cascudo, Luis da Câmara. *Literatura oral no Brazil*. São Paulo: Ed. Itatiaia, 1984.

Donato, Hernâni. *Contos dos meninos índios*. São Paulo: Melhoramentos, 1994.

Espinosa, Aurélia M. *Cuentos populares españoles*. Madrid: S. Aguirre, 1946.

Gomes, Lindolfo. *Contos populares brasileiros*. São Paulo: Melhoramentos, 1948.

Hartt, Charles Frederik. *Os mitos amazônicas da tartaruga*. Recife: Arquivo Público Estadual, 1952.

Koch-Grünberg, Theodor. *Von Roroima zum Orinoco*. Stuttgart: Strecker und Schröeder, 1924.

Laval, Ramón Arminio. *Cuentos de Pedro de Urdemalas*. Santiago de Chile: Cruz del Sur, 1943.

Magalhães, José Vieira Couto de. *O selvagem*. São Paulo: Melhoramentos, 1994.

Pereira, Nunes. *Moronguetá: Um decameron indígena*. Rio de Janeiro: Civilizaçào Brasileria, 1967.

Silva, Alberto da Costa. *Antologia de lendas do índi brasileiro*. Rio de Janeiro: INL, 1957.

INDEX

ABOUT THE AUTHORS

Livia de Almeida is a journalist and editor of *Veja Rio,* a weekly magazine, for which she writes on art, children's entertainment, and food. She discovered stories in the most traditional way, by listening to the tales that her grandfather told every night when she was a child; and later rediscovered storytelling with the help of her children, Luiz, Bernardo, and Isabel. Through a workshop done at the Casa da Leitura, in Rio, she came to recognize storytelling as an art form and to treasure folktales and the oral tradition. She has been a member of Mil e Umas storytelling troupe since 1996.

Ana Maria Portella, who was educated as a librarian, is a specialist in reading theory and practice at the Catholic University of Rio de Janeiro. She began storytelling after taking a workshop ten years ago and hasn't stopped since. Today she is a member of Mil e Umas storytelling troupe and volunteers in a day care center for children from the favelas (slums).

ABOUT THE EDITOR

Margaret Read MacDonald is an internationally renowned storyteller and author of more than forty-five books on folklore and storytelling. Margaret and Livia de Almeida did tandem storytelling at Rio's Tellabration in Brazil. Later Livia came to Seattle, Washington, to perform. From their shared enjoyment of story came this book. MacDonald has collaborated on folklore collections with Supaporn Vathanaprida (Thailand), Murti Bunanta (Indonesia), and Elvia Perez (Cuba). She is currently working on collections with Paula Martin (Argentina), Wajuppa Tossa and Kongduane Nattavong (Laos), and Nadiah Taibah (Saudi Arabia).

Recent Titles in the World Folklore Series

Additional titles in this series can be found at www.lu.com